Teach Now
Physical Educ......

The companion website for this series can be found at **www.routledge.com/cw/teachnow**. All of the useful web links highlighted in the book can be found here, along with additional resources and activities.

Being taught by a great teacher is one of the great privileges of life. Teach Now! is an exciting series that opens up the secrets of great teachers and, step by step, helps trainees, or teachers new to the profession, to build the skills and confidence they need to become first-rate classroom practitioners.

Written by a highly-skilled practitioner, this accessible guide contains all the support you need to become a great Physical Education teacher. Combining a grounded, modern rationale for teaching with highly practical training approaches, the book offers clear, straightforward advice on effective practice which will develop students' physical literacy, knowledge and inter-personal skills.

Enhanced by carefully chosen examples to demonstrate good practice, and with key definitions and ready-to-use activities included throughout, the book examines the aims and value of teaching PE, and outlines the essential components of providing a good Physical Education to students of all ages and abilities. Planning, assessment and behaviour management are all covered in detail, alongside chapters which focus upon the criteria and objectives of an effective PE curriculum, how to support students with special educational needs and physical disabilities, and how to create practical and effective ways to cater for the most-able students within PE.

Teach Now! Physical Education contains all the support required by trainee or newly qualified PE teachers. With advice on job applications, interviews, and your very first term, this book is your essential guide as you start your exciting career as an outstanding Physical Education teacher.

Daniel Burton currently teaches at King Edward VI School in Bury St Edmunds as Director of Sport and Student Leadership. He is involved in training NQTs and trainees from a range of providers, embedding student leadership across the school and helping to develop teaching and learning.

Teach Now!

Series editor: Geoff Barton

Being taught by a great teacher is one of the genuine privileges of life. *Teach Now!* is an exciting new series that opens up the secrets of great teachers and, step-by-step, helps trainees and new recruits to the profession to build the skills and confidence they need to become first-rate classroom practitioners. The series comprises a core text that explores what every teacher needs to know about essential issues such as learning, pedagogy, assessment and behaviour management, and subject-specific books that guide the reader through the key components and challenges in teaching individual subjects. Written by expert practitioners, the books in this series combine an underpinning philosophy of teaching and learning alongside engaging activities, strategies and techniques to ensure success in the classroom.

Titles in the series:

Teach Now! The Essentials of Teaching
What You Need to Know to Be a Great Teacher
Geoff Barton

Teach Now! Physical Education
Becoming a Great PE Teacher
Daniel Burton

Teach Now! Modern Foreign Languages
Becoming a Great Teacher of Modern Foreign Languages
Sally Allan

Teach Now! Mathematics
Becoming a Great Mathematics Teacher
Julia Upton

Teach Now! Science
The Joy of Teaching Science
Tom Sherrington

Teach Now! English
Becoming a Great English Teacher
Alex Quigley

Teach Now!
Physical Education

Becoming a Great PE Teacher

Daniel Burton

Routledge
Taylor & Francis Group

LONDON AND NEW YORK

First published 2018
by Routledge
2 Park Square, Milton Park, Abingdon, Oxon OX14 4RN

and by Routledge
711 Third Avenue, New York, NY 10017

Routledge is an imprint of the Taylor & Francis Group, an informa business

© 2018 Daniel Burton

British Library Cataloguing-in-Publication Data
A catalogue record for this book is available from the British Library

Library of Congress Cataloging-in-Publication Data
A catalog record for this book has been requested

ISBN: 978-1-138-08033-1 (hbk)
ISBN: 978-1-138-08034-8 (pbk)
ISBN: 978-1-315-11352-4 (ebk)

Typeset in Celeste and Optima
by Florence Production Ltd, Stoodleigh, Devon, UK

Visit the companion website: www.routledge.com/cw/teachnow

Contents

Contents

Series editor's foreword

What is this series about, and who is it for?

Many of us unashamedly like being teachers.

We shrug off the jibes about being in it for the holidays. We ignore the stereotypes in soap operas, sitcoms, bad films and serious news programmes. We don't feel any need to apologise for what we do, despite a constant and corrosive sense of being undervalued.

We always knew that being criticised was part of the deal.

We aren't defensive. We aren't apologetic. We simply like teaching.

And, whether we still spend the majority of our working week in the classroom, or as senior leaders, we regard the classroom as a sanctuary from the swirling madness beyond the school gates, we think teaching matters.

We think it matters a lot.

And we think that students need more good teachers.

That's where 'Teach Now!' started as a concept. Could we – as a group of teachers and teaching leaders, scattered across England – put together the kind of books we wish we had had when we were embarking on our own journeys into the secret garden of education?

Of course, there were lots of books around then. Nowadays there are even more – books, plus ebooks, blogs and tweets. You can hardly move on the Internet without tripping over another reflection on a lesson that went well or badly, another teacher extolling a particular approach, or dismissing another craze, or moaning about the management.

So we know you don't necessarily think you need us. There are plenty of people out there ready to shovel advice and guidance towards a fledgling teacher.

But we wanted to do something different. We wanted to provide two essential texts that would distil our collective knowledge as teachers and package it in a form that was easy to read, authoritative, re-readable, reassuring and deeply rooted in the day-to-day realities of education as it is – not as a consultant or adviser might depict it.

We are writing, in other words, in the early hours of days when each of us will be teaching classes, taking assemblies, watching lessons, looking at schemes of work and dealing with naughty students – and possibly naughty teachers.

We believe this gives our series a distinctive sense of being grounded in the realities of real schools, the kind of places we each work in every day.

We want to provide a warts-and-all account of how to be a great teacher, but we also each believe that education is an essentially optimistic career.

However grim the news out there, in our classrooms we can weave a kind of magic, given the right conditions and the right behaviour. We can reassure ourselves and the students in front of us that, together, we can make the world better.

And if that seems far-fetched, then you haven't seen enough great teachers.

As Roy Blatchford – himself an exceptional teacher and now the Director of the National Education Trust – says in his list of what great teachers do:

> The best teachers are children at heart.
> Sitting in the best lessons, you just don't want to leave.
> (Roy Blatchford, *The 2012 Teachers' Standards in the Classroom*, Sage, 2013)

We want young people to experience more lessons like that – in classrooms where the sense of time is different, where it expands and shrinks as the world beyond the classroom recedes, and where interest and passion and fascination take over; places where, whatever your background, your brain will fire with new experiences, thoughts and ideas; where, whatever your experience so far of the adult world, here, in this classroom, is an adult who cares a lot about something, can communicate it vividly and, in the way she or he talks and behaves, demonstrates a care and interest in you that is remarkable.

We need more classrooms like that and more teachers to take their place within them.

So that's what we have set out to do: to create a series of books that will – if you share our sense of moral purpose – help you to become a great teacher.

You'll have noticed that we expect you to buy two books. We said we were optimistic. That's because we think that being a great teacher has two important dimensions to it. First, you need to know your subject – to really know it.

We know, from very good sources, that the most effective teachers are experts in what they teach. That doesn't mean they know everything about it. In fact, they often fret about how little they feel they truly know. But they are hungry and passionate and eager – and all those other characteristics that define the teachers who inspire us.

So we know that subject knowledge is really important – and not just for teaching older students. It is as important when teaching Year 7s, knowing what you need to teach and what you can, for now, ignore.

We also believe that subject knowledge is much more than a superficial whisk through key dates or key concepts. It's about having a depth of knowledge that allows us to join up ideas, to explore complexity and nuance, to make decisions about what the key building-blocks of learning a subject might be.

Series editor's foreword

Great teachers sense this and, over a number of years, they build their experience and hone their skills. That's why we have developed subject specialist books for English, mathematics, history, modern foreign languages, science and physical education. These are the books that will help you to take what you learned on your degree course and to think through how to make that knowledge and those skills powerfully effective in the classroom.

They will take you from principles to practice, from philosophy deep into pedagogy. They will help to show you that any terror you may have about becoming a teacher of a subject is inevitable, and that knowing your stuff, careful planning, informed strategies – all of these will help you to teach now.

Then there's *Teach Now! The Essentials of Teaching*, which is the core text because we also believe that, even if you are the best informed scientist, linguist or mathematician in the universe, this in itself won't make you a great teacher.

That's because great teachers do things that support and supplement their subject knowledge. This is the stuff that the late great educator Michael Marland called the 'craft of the classroom'. It's what the best teachers know and do instinctively, but, to those of us looking on from the outside, or in the earliest stages of a teaching career, can seem mysterious, unattainable, a kind of magic.

It's also the kind of stuff that conventional training may not sufficiently cover.

We're talking about how to open the classroom door, knowing where to stand, knowing what to say to the student who is cheeky, knowing how to survive when you feel, in the darkest of glooms and intimidated by preparation and by marking, that you have made a terrible career choice.

These two texts combined – the subject specialist book and the core book – are designed to help you wherever you are training – in a school or academy or on a PGCE course. Whether you are receiving expert guidance, or it's proving to be more mixed, we hope our ideas, approaches and advice will reassure you and help you to gain in confidence.

We hope we are providing books that you will want to read and re-read as you train, as you take up your first post, and as you finally shrug off the feelings of early insecurity and start to stretch your wings as a fully fledged teacher.

So that's the idea behind the books.

And throughout the writing of them we have been very conscious that – just like us – you have too little time. We have therefore aimed to write in a style that is easy to read, reassuring, occasionally provocative and opinionated. We don't want to be bland: teaching is too important for any of us to wilt under a weight of colourless eduspeak.

That's why we have written in short paragraphs, short chapters, added occasional points for reflection and discussion and comments from trainee and veteran teachers, and aimed throughout to create practical, working guides to help you teach now.

So thanks for choosing to read what we have provided. We would love to hear how your early journey into teaching goes and hope that our series helps you on your way into and through a rewarding and enjoyable career.

Geoff Barton
with Sally Allan, Daniel Burton, Mike Gershon,
Alex Quigley, Tom Sherrington and Julia Upton
The *Teach Now!* team of authors

Acknowledgements

I would like to thank the series editor of 'Teach Now!', Geoff Barton, for presenting me with the opportunity to contribute to this series. You have believed in me to promote the outcomes which derive from this subject – and for that I am eternally grateful. Thank you for being a great leader, mentor and friend.

I would also like to thank all of the people that have supported me throughout my career, from those who inspired me within my own educational journey, to those who have worked alongside me within my current role in education.

Finally, I would like to thank everyone who has supported me in the completion of this book. From proof reading, editing and producing final manuscripts, to motivation and encouragement. I am so pleased to have had this opportunity and hope it will be used to inspire the next generation of PE teachers.

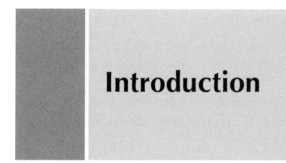

Introduction

Why become a teacher of Physical Education?

In recent years, there has been a significant increase in the number of people who want to become a PE teacher. But what is it about teaching PE that makes it a popular career within secondary education?

It is a chance to have an enjoyable occupation within sport. For some, it may be an attractive career choice if competing within sport yourself is not an option. For others, it may be that just having the opportunity to share your passion for sport is your motivation to join the profession.

Teaching PE presents a great opportunity to inspire the next generation of students to be healthier and more active, among many other key skills.

Before deciding to embark on a career within this subject, it is important to understand what Physical Education is.

This question can be answered in three sections:

1. developing physical skills;
2. improving knowledge; and
3. nurturing inter-personal skills.

Developing physical skills

All students should leave education with a physical skill set which will enable them to participate in a range of activities which are of interest to them.

It is important to develop these skills within a wide range of activity areas to increase the probability of the students pursuing a sport within their own time.

This is known as developing 'physical literacy' – a term used to describe students mastering the fundamental movement and sport-specific skills in order to confidently participate in sport and physical activity.

Improving knowledge

Students will need to understand how their body works; how their body changes while participating in physical activities, and the benefits which derive from exercise over a long period of time.

Knowledge will also need to be developed within particular sporting activities – for example rules, strategies, tactics and understanding how to effectively perform a skill to name a few.

One of the key elements of developing knowledge, however, is enabling our students to make informed decisions about their lifestyle:

- How much do you need to exercise to have a positive impact on your health?
- How do you ensure that you are exercising safely?
- How often should you exercise?
- What do you need to do in order to improve your health or fitness?

Students will develop this knowledge over time, throughout their educational journey – it does not need to be explicitly taught, but must remain an important outcome of Physical Education.

Nurturing inter-personal skills

As well as the skill development and knowledge mentioned above, we must also consider the other skills which are developed through PE. This is one of the main strengths of our subject, and is what makes it unique to other subjects within the students' curriculum.

Students will need to develop a range of skills to prepare them for life outside of their education – this is known as 'lifelong learning'. What additional skills do you think can be developed through an effective PE curriculum?

Consider skills such as communication – being able to communicate with others is an essential skill in most careers and is developed within PE.

This will include: Speaking and listening skills, body language, as well as written and verbal communication which will also be developed within a classroom environment.

Solving problems and collaborating with others are other examples of inter-personal skills which are derived from sport and PE.

Why did I become a PE teacher?

I have been one of the lucky ones in relation to having the opportunity to teach this subject – I have always been passionate about sport, and this career has given me an excellent platform to promote that to a large number of young people.

But why teach? Why did I not choose to pursue a career in coaching my favourite sport? Or work within elite sport?

Try to recall your earliest memories of PE within your education – what did PE look like to you then?

I can remember the uncomfortable PE kits – the short shorts, plimsolls and gym tops we were all made to wear. The sound of a whistle bellowing across the small gymnasium. The long lines we were ordered to stand in while waiting for a turn at performing on some apparatus.

Introduction

PE has changed a lot since my education – and I wanted to be part of that change.

Eradicating long lines of people and waiting around to have my turn is now a key part of an effective PE lesson. PE kits are now designed to allow students to feel comfortable within a practical environment, to be more motivated, and proud to wear the kits as part of their school community.

But the biggest reason for me choosing a career within PE is the opportunity I now have to inspire others to enjoy PE and sport – increasing a student's confidence to try things outside of their comfort zone, and the satisfaction of seeing students enjoying physical activity.

What is it which interests, or interested you in becoming a PE teacher?

The 'anatomy' of PE teaching

Throughout this book, I will make reference to a variety of teaching strategies, with applied examples, to aid your development as a PE teacher early on in your career.

What this book will not do is prescribe a range of lessons and strategies for you to follow – this is not teaching. What you include in your lessons on a day-to-day basis is entirely up to you.

Over time you will become familiar with your classes, you will know what strategies work well, and what things do not – but every class will be different.

Try to use some of the ideas outlined within this book to apply to your teaching. Experiment with different strategies and do not be afraid to do things differently. The important part of this process is being able to reflect, and adapt accordingly for future lessons.

Some aspects presented in this book will need to be embedded into your teaching routines, such as assessment strategies and questioning. Although this concept will need to be present, how you achieve it can be your decision.

My advice early on in your career would be to keep a basic and constant structure to your lessons at first. Gain confidence within your basic teaching episodes, such as warm ups, giving instructions and sorting a class into smaller teams for small-sided games.

Once you have gained some experience and confidence, you can start to place your own ideas into practice – but remember to continually reflect on your teaching and adapt accordingly when needed.

Be sure to explore the different ways in which students learn within PE. Trial some group work, reciprocal tasks or creative ways to answer a question within a practical environment.

How to use this book

This book has been produced as a companion, to guide trainee or recently qualified teachers through some of the factors which will contribute to the effective teaching of Physical Education.

It aims to provide detailed support and guidance within a number of teaching topics – from deciding what activities to teach, to assessing your classes within lessons.

Each chapter includes some definitions, explanations, but most importantly contains some practical examples from the subject which apply the theory to practice.

Try to use each example yourself, apply the ideas within your planning, review your own teaching regularly – and eventually make your teaching your own.

My final words of advice before you begin to use this book . . . don't be afraid to take risks with your teaching. Try to be different, and try things which are distinctive. Be sure to consider the needs of the students you are teaching within these processes and enjoy your teaching – there are very few careers which allow an individual to directly influence a young person's passion for sport.

I hope you enjoy this practical guide to becoming a great PE teacher. I also hope you enjoy a career as rewarding and challenging as I have.

1 The aims of Physical Education

Before you can begin to understand the mechanics of becoming a PE teacher, it is important that you have an understanding of what PE is, and why it is an important subject for schools to include within their curriculum.

The subject has developed a lot since the 1940s, when it was transformed into an educational subject from its earlier physical recreational form. But what are the aims of Physical Education in our schools today?

It is always an interesting process to see what student's opinions are. Here are some responses to the question above:

'To achieve in areas of sport that are personal to yourself.'

'PE is important for becoming fit, developing teamwork and relaxing (time away from academic studies).'

'PE is about teamwork and working on yourself, it can have an impact on your mind, not just your body.'

'Teaching not only physical well-being but teaching multiple vital life skills through the form of physical activity and biological study.'

'For some, to step out of their comfort zone and achieve what they thought couldn't be possible!'

As you can see, this question is always answered with a vast array of responses – which highlights the multiple benefits derived from Physical Education.

But what are the definitive aims of Physical Education?

This question has two possible answers: one related to the outcomes expected from the National Curriculum, and the other being the general aims of the subject which have an overriding impact on student's health and well-being.

Aims of the National Curriculum for PE (NCPE)

There have been a variety of reforms and changes made to the NCPE, including the aims and expected outcomes which derive from the subject.

That being said, there are also some consistent 'themes' that are present. These will need to be considered when planning to teach PE, and developments made by our students towards these aims should be assessed to show their progress.

The current aims of PE at Key Stage 3 (11 to 14 years old) and Key Stage 4 (14 to 16 years old) can be split into the following categories:

- **Building on previous learning**: It is important that lessons within secondary school PE build upon the students' previous learning.

    You do not need to have an in-depth understanding of the earlier Key Stages, but you will require a basic knowledge of what fundamental skills your students will have developed.

    This should include mastering movements such as running, jumping, throwing and catching. As well as developing their fitness, such as balance, agility and co-ordination.

- **Development of skills**: PE within Key Stages 1 and 2 includes the development of fundamental skills, such as running, throwing and catching.

These will need further development, such as applying these skills to sport-specific skills. For example, progressing 'throwing and catching' movements to aiming a cricket ball towards a set of cricket stumps.

This will later progress to developing basic skills within a wide range of activities. This should increase the probability of your students taking part in this sport outside of PE lessons.

This theme will also include the development of fitness. PE will need to develop the physical capacity of our students by improving a range of fitness components, such as stamina and strength.

- **Making and applying decisions**: As students become more confident performing the skills they have developed, within certain sporting contexts, they will then need to advance their understanding of the activity they are undertaking.

  This will include teaching students when to appropriately apply these learnt skills within a competitive situation.

  For example, following the development of a basic lateral pass in rugby, students will then need to understand when to time their passes to be effective against an opponent.

- **Evaluate and improve**: With a greater understanding of skills and techniques, your students should be taught how to analyse themselves, or others when performing.

  This could later include analysing different tactics and strategies within competitive games – which will require further knowledge of the activity they are undertaking.

  Within this theme, students should also develop other inter-personal skills. These include problem solving and communication.

- **Making informed decisions which influence the student's health and well-being**: This outcome is associated with the skills that the students require to be able to make decisions regarding their own health.

Students will need to learn about the effects of exercise and physical activity. This will include knowledge of how to participate safely.

Once students have acquired the skills and knowledge of an activity, they should then be provided with the information they need to further pursue that activity if it is of interest to them.

General aims of PE within secondary schools

Although all of the above aims are outlined within the NCPE, Physical Education has many additional benefits which are not overtly outlined, but still from an important part for the aims of PE.

Below are some examples of the skills we expect to derive for PE within secondary schools:

- **Increasing confidence/self-esteem**: One of the fundamental aims of PE is to increase confidence for our students.

  Students should be provided a platform to confidently conduct their work in increasingly challenging situations – which will require them to be confident within their own abilities.

  This will allow pupils within your lessons to perform practical skills in front of others, take risks and pursue activities in their own time.

- **Mental health benefits**: In addition to improving our students' self-confidence, there are a number of other mental health benefits which can be derived from an effective PE curriculum.

  This includes teaching our students how to manage stress levels, and gaining an understanding of how exercise/physical activity can support this.

The aims of Physical Education

PE also provides an opportunity for less academic students to achieve success within an educational requirement, which will have its own mental health benefits, including an increased engagement within school.

- **Enjoyment**: This aim is very self-explanatory, but remains an important aim.

PE needs to be enjoyable, particularly if we want to engage students that are 'switched-off' from sport or physical activity.

If students are actively enjoying the subject, or the activity they are being taught, they are also more likely to pursue this in the future.

- **Developing creativity**: Sport and PE provide many opportunities for students to invent outcomes.

Whether this is using creative methods to express ideas within a dance, or outwitting an opponent on the sports field, creativity is an important skill we need to develop.

This concept is one that sets our subject apart from other academic subjects. Creativity is a characteristic which many other countries are beginning to put more focus upon within education as they look at developing their future workforce.

- **Sportsmanship**: This refers to the ability of our students to enjoy competitive activities for what they are.

This includes their ability to compete fairly, within the rules and boundaries of the sport or activity. Respecting your team mates and opponents will be an important part of this aim.

Teaching our students to win gracefully, and show our opponents courtesy within defeat are important components of an athlete's mentality, and we will need to encourage this within our lessons.

- **Introducing students to a wide range of activities**: The breadth of study that students have been introduced to will directly influence the probability of them pursuing activities in the future.

A PE curriculum which only contains a small number of activities may not effectively engage students to the point that they will want to develop their skills further, or join a community club to access further challenges.

In the past, the NCPE has been descriptive to ensure students are given a broad number of activities, from different activity areas. This has included activity areas such as invasion games (e.g. football or netball), net/wall games (e.g. tennis), and communicating concepts/ideas (e.g. dance or gymnastics).

This has now been removed to empower teachers to make more decisions for the classes they are teaching, therefore allowing us to provide a bespoke curriculum which will engage our students.

It is important that we provide a wide range of activities, from different activity areas to give our students as many experiences as we can within curriculum PE lessons.

- **Promoting and improving health/fitness**: PE is the foundation level of physical participation. It is within schools that most students will learn fundamental skills required to access sport and physical activities later in life.

  Students also need to gain an understanding of what a healthy lifestyle is, and how the decisions they make can influence their health.

  Providing students with PE also creates approximately two hours per week of activity. It is an important aim to ensure that this time is purposeful, and providing students an opportunity to be active.

  Other secondary aims within this theme include supporting the physical growth and development of young people. Factors such as posture and core strength can be influenced significantly by PE, and should form part of the aims of the subject.

- **Producing/supporting elite performers**: Another aim of a successful PE programme will be to support students at whatever ability level they are currently within.

The aims of Physical Education

PE is an important part of an athlete's development – it provides students with the fundamental skills to access sport early in their educational journey.

There may be students present within your classes who perform at a high-standard within a sport. Supporting these students is an important aim.

A PE teacher generally has a good understanding of the support needed for students who perform at a high level.

Interventions and support will need to be available within PE lessons, and may be required outside of the subject with a whole-school focus, such as teaching the students to balance their studies with training commitments.

- **Physical literacy**: This term refers to developing all of the necessary fundamental skills which are required to access physical activities.

  Capability to perform physical activity for prolonged periods of time will be an important factor if students wish to apply their skills to physical activities, while also having obvious advantages to their general health.

  Students need to be capable of accessing sport. For example, without co-ordination, how would a student be able to perform a rally within a basic badminton lesson?

  Physical literacy should not only be related to PE and Sport however. Students who may wish to pursue careers which are strenuous or physically demanding will also require these fundamental skills, learnt initially via their PE curriculum.

- **Leadership**: This is a vague term which can include many components.

  But at the core, leadership requires students to be capable of a number of inter-personal skills which can be developed through PE.

  These could include communication, organisation and problem solving. All skills which can be easily translated to other subjects and careers.

- **Lifelong learning**: This aim relates to our students being given the appropriate and necessary skills and abilities which can contribute to whatever they pursue later in life.

    This could include a number of employability skills which are developed within PE, such as communication skills or determination.

    This aim also relates directly to ensuring our students have the appropriate physical capabilities to participate in sport beyond curriculum PE.

These aims are not restricted to the ones listed above, and every PE teacher will have their own opinion on what the additional aims of the subject are.

There are some alternative aspects you also need to consider, such as ensuring physical activity remains at an appropriate level and how your role as a PE teacher differs from that of a sports coach.

Education, not to the detriment of physical activity

It must not be forgotten that one of the major aims of PE is to improve health.

Every PE lesson within a practical environment needs to ensure that the students are actively participating, and where possible are taking part in activities that are vigorous and challenging.

Educating students about safety implications or anatomy are important, but need to be built in to lessons so that physical activity is not reduced.

Consider a PE lesson where a majority of the time is directed towards discussions: Are these lessons enjoyable? Will these lessons inspire students to take part in physical activity within their own time?

Finding a balance between physical activity and developing theoretical knowledge is difficult to achieve early on in your teaching career, and some guidance to help you achieve this will be outlined later within this book.

PE teacher vs sports coach

It is common to see a number of newly qualified teachers enter the profession from a coaching background, or at least have some sports coaching experience. But is this enough experience to make you an effective PE teacher?

Sports coaches tend to work with students/athletes that are highly self-motivated. Consider how you will effectively deal with students who are disengaged from sport – how will you motivate them to take part confidently?

A coach may also use a repetitive style of coaching to allow students to master a specific skill. Drills and activities will be repeated numerous times until the desired outcome is achieved: Would this strategy be effective within a secondary school PE lesson? Or could it create boredom which may result in some behaviour issues?

Being a sports coach does however develop a deep understanding of a specific sport. This is useful subject knowledge which can be applied to teaching. It will enable you to critically analyse a student's performance, and have a good understanding of how the student can improve.

However, this alone will not be adequate and make you an effective PE teacher. You will require knowledge of a wide range of activities and theory concepts.

Do you have a range of strategies which can be used to support a student who maybe struggling to perform a specific skill? Would you know when a skill or performance has been produced well and have the knowledge to challenge these students further?

Ideally, you will want to have the physical capacity to demonstrate most skills to aid your students understanding of a task or skill.

Values and visions

An important consideration you should make when considering the aims of PE within the school you are working in, is the aims and values of the school itself.

Does Physical Education contribute to the whole-school aims and values?

Another important aim for a PE programme within your school will be how effectively you can link the outcomes of your lessons to the school's, or department's overall vision.

This can often take the form of a 'mission statement' or set of values, but must also contribute to the aims of PE within the school.

It may be that certain aims listed earlier in this chapter need to be more explicitly taught and assessed in-line with your school's objectives.

For example, if you are working in a school which has strong religious connections, such as a Catholic School, or Church of England School, it might be that PE can be used more to compliment the school's ethos.

Highlighting more overtly the impact PE has on sportsmanship, or respect of others are examples of how this can be effective.

But, how about using arguably the most powerful values in sport to inspire students within Physical Education – the Olympic and Paralympic values?

Inspiring others – the Olympic legacy

PE also plays an important part in exemplifying the kind of values and behaviours we want in society – those enshrined in the Olympics and then modelled in schools.

Very few people understand the rationale for reviving the Olympic Games back in 1896.

French educator Pierre de Coubertin was the mastermind behind the re-introduction of the Olympic Games (or what we know as the modern Olympic Games), and this all stemmed from the school sports systems in place within Britain.

The aims of Physical Education

De Coubertin was convinced that a highly structured school sports system, which was governed by students would improve people's perceptions of physical activity – and at this time have the effect of improving the health, fitness and discipline of those enlisted within the French Army.

However, one of the key products of De Coubertin's work was the creation of the Olympic, and Paralympic values. These can be very easily applied to the values of PE, and can be used to inspire our students within lessons.

Below are the Olympic and Paralympic values, with an example of an application to PE:

The Olympic values

- **Respect**: Developing an understanding of sportsmanship for our students, playing by the rules, and learning to win and lose competition in the right way.

- **Excellence**: Students trying their best within a task, however challenging it may be to begin with. This could also include supporting students who compete at a high standard.

- **Friendship**: Promoting inter-personal skills such as empathy, trust and teamwork. This can be very easily linked to most team sports.

The Paralympic values

- **Determination**: Developing resilience within our students, encouraging students to keep on trying if they find something difficult, and persevering.

- **Inspiration**: Using role models linked to a particular activity, skill and personality trait. Better still, being a positive role model yourself, or developing your students to be role models to others.

- **Courage**: Developing self-confidence within our students to allow them to effectively take risks.

- **Equality**: Treating others as equals. Teaching students about discrimination and prejudice is important, and can be effectively taught within the PE environment.

It is not only these values that can be used as a tool to inspire young people. Consider the Olympic Games hosted in London – one of the key characteristics which made these games a success was the work produced by volunteers.

This is a powerful message to young people, and can be used to motivate them to perform in physical activities, or contribute to PE and school sport within different capacities, such as leaders or organisers.

These values can very easily be related to Physical Education, and can effectively guide schools, departments and students towards successful outcomes.

Better examples of this are schools which have created their own values. You will need to discover these before you start working in a school to ensure they are embedded in your teaching – ensuring PE and school sport contribute to the 'heartbeat' of your school.

CHAPTER SUMMARY

- Consider why PE is an important subject for schools to keep within their taught curriculum.
- PE has many aims, which can be split into two categories: aims of the NCPE, and more general outcomes.
- You need to ensure you meet the required aims of the NCPE, these are statutory.
- The other more general outcomes are not less important, but are values which derive from a successful PE programme.
- Consider the values or vision of the school you are working in – can you link the aims of PE to the whole-school aims?

TALKING POINTS

1. What does Physical Education mean to you?
2. Why do you feel its place in a school's curriculum is important?
3. What is it about being a PE teacher that you are most excited or daunted by?
4. Which ideas, concepts or topics in PE are the ones you're really looking forward to sharing with the students in your classes?

2 Curriculum essentials in Physical Education

This chapter will break down the key concepts within the National Curriculum for PE. This will include discussing the main principles associated with the Key stage 3 and 4 curriculums, including:

- What activities to teach
- What a 'good' PE curriculum should include
- How to assess your students
- The expected learning outcomes.

Later in this chapter, guidance will be outlined for teaching examination courses, such as GCSE PE. This will include:

- Practical assessments
- Teaching the theory elements of the course
- Teaching theory content within practical lessons
- Preparation for the theory examination.

Key skills which form part of our subject's uniqueness will also be referred to throughout this chapter. This will include practical advice with ways to develop these skills within your lessons.

Key Stage 3 Physical Education

As a 'core' subject, schools should aim to provide students with at least two hours of curriculum PE per week, as well as activities which supplement this out-of-school hours.

This time commitment provides an excellent platform for us as PE teachers to make an impact upon students' physical development – but is it enough to create your country's next Olympian?

The outcomes of a good PE curriculum are twofold: to increase the knowledge and understanding of how to maintain a healthy, active lifestyle and to improve physical literacy.

The term 'physical literacy' refers to the development of fundamental skills which students can then use within different activities and contexts. An effective PE programme should allow students to confidently produce skills and make decisions in a wide range of physical activity situations.

Therefore, the most effective curriculums have to be those which consist of a variety of activities, from a range of areas.

What activities do you need to teach?

The current National Curriculum for PE at Key Stage 3 (published September 2013) does not give much direction towards activities that need to be taught – here is a summary of what needs to be delivered:

- Skills, tactics and strategies in team and individual games (for example, badminton, basketball, cricket, football, tennis, etc.).
- Develop technique and performance in other competitive sports (for example, gymnastics and athletics).
- A range of dance styles and forms (for example, contemporary dance and physical theatre).
- Outdoor and adventurous activities (for example, orienteering, problem solving, mountaineering, etc.).

These activity areas are deliberately vague to allow us to create bespoke curriculum programmes based around the needs of our own students.

The challenge is to then use this empowerment to devise a curriculum that is not only effective, but engaging to all students. Introducing a range of activities to our students increases the chances of them pursuing these in their own time – and developing physical literacy and transferable skills will allow them to do this confidently.

Decisions will need to be made regarding the amount of time which is spent delivering each activity and what activities need to be taught.

The danger of this empowerment is that curriculums are constructed with the teacher's expertise at the centre – and not the student's needs. It is important to ensure students are subjected to a broad 'diet' for the reasons already outlined.

Activities such as dance can be an activity which is side-lined within many male PE programmes due to pre-judgements – but the advantages of delivering this activity well outweigh its sometimes negative impressions.

Development of creativity, flexibility and core-strength to name only a few benefits of delivering this activity – not to mention taking some students outside of their usual comfort zone.

Assessment

Assessment in PE has always had issues which need to be considered – including its subjective nature and what elements of the subject need to be assessed. Therefore, it is important to return to the rationale for assessing students in the first place.

Assessment should be used as a method of displaying the progress a student is making – allowing them to use this information for further development, not just as a summative result of a unit of work.

Moving away from assessments at the end of teaching an activity area will allow the students to use this information continually, and make improvements – known in the teaching profession as 'Assessment for Learning'.

There is still a need, however, to ensure that some element of formal assessment is conducted for a number of reasons – information to parents/guardians, report writing and suitability for Key Stage 4 subjects to name a few.

But how can this be done effectively, and consistently across different teaching groups and staff?

The use of generic assessment tasks can be a good way to ensure students are assessed in a similar way between teaching groups, using some agreed criteria of what is being assessed.

Example 1: If assessing a Year 7 class, it may be that judgements are being made in their ability to replicate activity specific skills in isolation. An in-step pass football, a shot in netball or a forward roll in gymnastics.

Example 2: If assessing a Year 9 class, it may be the appropriate application of skills within increasingly challenging environments which need to be assessed. Application of passing and control techniques in invasion games, or the application of different choreographic devises in dance.

A helpful resource to consider is working with your colleagues for collaborative assessments. Using time to discuss assessments with other PE specialists improves the consistency of assessments, and provides a great platform for developmental discussions.

The expected learning outcomes

Although the PE curriculum can be bespoke in relation to the activities being delivered, there are a number of clear outcomes our subject needs to develop.

1. **Fundamental skills**: These can be sport-specific in certain situations, but the most effective are those which can be transferred between different activity areas.

    For example, students will need to be taught skills in isolation which can then be applied to activities – a forehand serve in Badminton, or a push pass in Hockey.

    Other fundamental skills could include movement skills such as a body feint which could then be applied to a number of invasion games.

2. **Knowledge and understanding of health/fitness**: students will need to gain an understanding of how the body responds to physical activity (short- and long-term effects) which can then be used to make informed decisions to improve their own health.

    Other outcomes include the importance of exercising safely – which includes basic risk assessments, and performing an effective warm up/cool down.

    This area also needs to ensure that students develop their physical capacity to perform skills and activities effectively – and develop an understanding of how to improve their performances via health and fitness gains.

3. **Skills, tactics and strategies**: Applying previously learnt skills to competitive situations. This area also includes applying strategies/tactics to overcome an opponent.

    For example, applying effective passing techniques in small sided games to maintain possession or performing specific set-plays within a competitive environment.

    This area will also need to consider the application of movement skills in creative activities – and allow students to apply advanced skills and ideas within performances.

4. **Intellectual/physical skills**: The development of generic skills which can be transferred into different contexts.

For example, students need the opportunity to develop skills such as communication, working with others, problem solving, leadership and creativity to name a few.

5. **Analysing performance**: Students need to develop an understanding of how a skill is improving, and make adjustments accordingly.

This could be in the form of providing others with feedback during tasks, or reviewing their own work. Students will need to learn to compare skills, tactics and techniques and suggests ways in which the work could be improved.

Another key objective of Physical Education is the influence it has on 'lifelong learning'.

Developing physical confidences in a range of activities increases the probability of students choosing to further develop and participate in these activities in their own time.

It is unrealistic to assume that an effective PE curriculum will produce professional athletes – there is neither the time, nor the knowledge/resources to do this.

However, what we do have is a platform to promote curiosity in different physical activities, and an opportunity to develop physical literacy and fitness so that students can make informed decisions about their own lifestyles.

Key Stage 4 Physical Education

Again, as a 'core' subject, schools should aim to provide students with at least two hours of curriculum PE per week, as well as activities which supplement this out-of-school hours.

This can differ at this Key Stage if students follow an examination course in Physical Education – which is most commonly an option subject within secondary schools.

The majority of the National Curriculum builds upon what is covered at Key Stage 3 – but with an emphasis on students being presented with more complex and demanding activities.

It is imperative that student engagement is at the heart of a Key Stage 4 PE curriculum – most behaviour issues in the subject occur at this stage of the student's education due to some negative perceptions of the subject.

The curriculum will need to build on previously learnt skills in the last Key Stage – but with increased difficulty.

Example 1: Transferring skills learnt in earlier gymnastics units to trampolining.

Fundamental skills such as core strength and flexibility can be further challenged when applied to this activity, and skills can be easily transferred such as the key concepts of flight.

Example 2: Application of previously learnt skills into full versions of the game.

In the previous Key Stage, students would have started to apply and select skills/tactics/strategies to competitive situations – this can be made more difficult when applying to the sport in its normal form – such as a full game of hockey, compared to small-sided versions.

Assessment

This can take many forms – dependent on your department or schools individual policies. However, it is still important to ensure that these highlight students' understanding as to how they can improve.

Once again, decisions need to be made as to what the assessments are taking into consideration, but a clear emphasis needs to be made to lifelong learning.

Linking units of work to local community sports clubs and activities can be very powerful when educating your students to make informed decisions about their lifestyles. Assessments will allow you to signpost students to community partners more effectively using the students' strengths and interests to help.

PE as an examination subject

Physical Education remains a popular GCSE choice for students within secondary schools – there are a number of examination boards which offer the subject, which all have slight differences.

Specifications, and assessments (both practical and theory) and controlled assessments need to be investigated when making a decision about which examination board to choose.

The specifications outline the content that needs to be taught throughout the course. This will include topics such as:

- Anatomy and physiology
- Diet
- Fitness
- Training
- Technology
- Leisure and recreation
- Schools and PE.

Practical assessments

These will differ between examination boards, but the basic principles remain consistent.

Activity areas are assessed as two components: the sport-specific skills in isolation, and application of these within competitive versions of the sport.

The skills that need to be demonstrated by students will be outlined in the specification, but most tend to be very similar. Below are two examples of the types of skills this may include:

Example 1: Basketball. The skills that need to be assessed could include:

- *Passing*: Chest, javelin, bounce, overhead
- *Receiving/intercepting a pass*: While stationary and moving, rebounding

- *Dribbling*: Using both hands, changing direction/speed, beating an opponent

- *Shooting*: Lay-up, jump shot, set shot, free throw

- *Footwork*: Stopping, pivoting, cutting, tracking.

Another section of the assessment would be the application of the skills into a competitive environment.

For basketball, this may include performing in a full version of the game, and displaying an understanding of tactics and strategies, which includes responding effectively to opponents.

Example 2: Artistic gymnastics. The skills that need to be assessed could include:

- *Jumps*: Tuck, pike, straddle, straight, twist

- *Turns*: Cartwheel, walkovers

- *Balances*: Handstand, headstand

- *Springs*: Handspring, headspring, round-off.

The application part of this activity may be the performance of a routine. This may be pre-determined by the examination board, or there will be guidance as to what the students need to perform.

Some of the examination boards require different forms of evidence for these assessments. This could include moderation visits, or students submitting video evidence of their practical work.

Another important consideration is checking what activities are included on the specification. For example, there has been a recent rise in students taking part in different martial arts disciplines, and you will need to check as to whether the examination board allows these to form part of the student's practical assessment.

Ratio of practical and theory teaching

This is something that is not outlined by examination boards and a decision that needs to be made by the teacher.

An easy answer to this would be to match the course weightings with time allocated. For example, a 60% practical course would be given 60% of the allocated timetabled time for practical work and assessments.

Recent reforms (September 2016) saw a number of examination boards increase the weighting of the theory components of the course – in most cases, a 60% weighting to theory.

Schools that provide GCSE in addition to non-examination PE (as a core subject) may be able to use the non-examination lessons to obtain the practical assessments, creating more time to focus on the theory aspects in the additional lessons.

Teaching theory topics practically

What our subject allows us to do is apply theoretical topics easily into practical applications. Therefore, a number of the topics to be studied can be taught within practical environments.

For example, when teaching the different methods of training, each lesson could see the class conducting a fitness session using each method.

Discussions would be needed to ensure the knowledge required for the examination is sufficient. This allows students that learn more easily in practical environments an opportunity to apply their understanding.

A follow-up lesson may be needed to ensure written work illustrates the understanding needed, and links to examination questions would be an effective way to achieve this.

Here are some more examples of theory concepts which could be conducted practically.

Example 1: Components of fitness – For each component of fitness, students need to perform the appropriate test to measure the component. They will then need to analyse the data, and highlight their strengths and weaknesses as a performer in their sport.

This lesson will also need to make reference to defining each component of fitness, and applying it appropriately to a sporting context:

- *Component of fitness*: Agility

- *Definition*: The ability to change direction at speed

- *Application*: A Rugby player side-stepping an opponent to avoid a tackle

- *Fitness test*: The Illinois Agility Run.

Example 2: Training zones – Students need to calculate their maximum heart rate (drawing upon prior knowledge). Using this, they need to calculate what heart rates are needed to work within their aerobic and anaerobic training zones.

Once calculated, students need to perform two activities while wearing a heart rate monitor with the aim of working in both training zones.

The students could use appropriate cardiovascular equipment such as treadmills, exercise bikes, etc. or this could be conducted via running activities.

This could be linked to recovery if the students were to monitor their recovery back to rest using the heart rate monitors.

Example 3: Types of competitions – Students are to plan and deliver a simple competition in a given format (league, knockout, ladder or combined competition).

Activities such as badminton or table tennis are effective as games, and can be shortened for the purpose of the lesson.

Following each competition, a discussion is needed to highlight the advantages and disadvantages of each type of competition.

Example 4: Types of movements – Students perform a dance routine that consists of the basic movements required in their specification (flexion, extension, rotation, adduction and abduction).

Students then devise their own short motif that includes all of the movements (or has a focus on a selection of them), and others identify when each movement is produced.

This can be taken further by including planes and axis of movement. Actual performance of these movements will aid the students understanding of each, and they will then need to discuss application of these movements to different sporting examples.

For example, can you apply each movement to an example within tennis?

Example 5: Lever systems – Using some basic hand weights (dumbbells), some movements are replicated to demonstrate each lever system.

First class lever: Tricep extension

Second class lever: Calf rises

Third class lever: Upward phase of a bicep curl

Students will then need to draw a basic diagram of each type of lever, labelling the effort, resistance (or load) and fulcrum.

Each class of lever can then be applied to sporting examples, and mechanical advantages can be discussed.

Using practical tasks to reinforce theoretical concepts can be a very effective strategy for teaching, and for revision.

Particular care would need to be made when transferring the knowledge of these practical lessons into students completing examination style questions.

CHAPTER SUMMARY

- Consider the needs of your students when creating a Key Stage 3 and 4 PE curriculum.
- Ensure the curriculum is engaging, and meets the intended learning outcomes.
- Make sure your assessments are continuous and communicate these with your classes to maximize the progress they can make.
- Link units of work to community partners to increase probability of students further pursuing activities within your curriculum programme.
- Investigate the different examination boards, and make an informed decision that meets the needs of your students.
- Try to teach theory topics within practical environments where possible.

TALKING POINTS

1. What skills and knowledge do you feel a student should have when they move to secondary school?
2. What skills and knowledge do you think are important to include within your teaching?
3. How can you create a curriculum that is engaging and purposeful?
4. What community partners can be readily available to contribute to your PE curriculum? And how can you engage them to work with you within your school?

3 Planning essentials

To ensure that our teaching is effective, thorough planning is essential. But what does effective planning look like within Physical Education?

Throughout this chapter, advice will be given on all aspects which you will need to consider when planning for teaching. This will be divided into three sub-sections:

1. Long-term planning (schemes of work/programmes of study)

2. Medium-term (units of work)

3. Short-term (individual lesson planning)

Long-term planning

This element of planning can sometimes be known as 'schemes of work' or 'programmes of study', but is centred around the breadth of activities and topics which are going to be delivered. This could be planning for a school year, or within a key stage.

In order to make informed decisions about what needs to be covered within your planning – references need to be made to the National Curriculum for PE.

The National Curriculum for PE (NCPE) has been in place since 1992, following the introduction of the National Curriculum framework in 1988. Since then, a number of reforms have been implemented, but the core elements are still consistent.

The most up-to-date version was produced by the Department for Education (September 2013). Here is a brief summary of the requirements for teaching PE at Key stages 3 (11–14) and 4 (15–16).

NCPE Key Stage 3

- Students should build on PE content covered throughout the previous key stages (1 and 2).

- Students should become competent and confident in producing skills, techniques and concepts, which can be applied to a range of physical activities.

- Students should be able to highlight what makes a performance successful, and use this information to inform their own/others' work.

- Students need to develop an understanding of the long-term benefits physical activity has on their health, and become confident/interested in getting involved in physical activities.

Within the NCPE, there is no obligation to cover specific sports activities such as football and netball. However, we do have an obligation to our students to ensure they cover a wide range of activities to increase the possibility of them pursuing sport/ physical activity outside of school.

The activities areas which are required to be covered as part of the NCPE include:

1. Outwitting opponents (e.g. football, netball, basketball, cricket, rounders, tennis, etc.)

2. Performing at maximal capacity (e.g. gymnastics and athletics)

3. Exploring concepts and ideas (such as dance – including a range of forms/styles)

4. Outdoor and adventurous activities (such as team building, problem solving and orienteering).

NCPE Key Stage 4

- Students should be able to confidently apply their skills within complex and demanding situations/activities.

- Students should cover a wide range of physical activities to develop their health, fitness and contribute to a healthy lifestyle.

As with Key Stage 3 PE, the breadth of study is important to maximize the potential of students pursuing activities further in their own time.

The activity areas remain the same, however, it is important at this stage of the student's education to develop more bespoke curriculum content to ensure students remain engaged and participate readily.

Using the framework of the NCPE, effective long-term planning can take place. However, one of the characteristics of our subject which differs from others is the need to use specific facilities in order to deliver certain activities.

This does however, more often than not, present an opportunity to empower PE teachers with the ability to decide which activities to deliver, and making these decisions with the students of the class in consideration.

What will need to be 'mapped' within the long-term planning is the learning outcomes which need to be delivered, in line with the NCPE.

For example, if the sports field is your facility for your first term, this presents you with approximately 12 weeks of curriculum time. A vast number of activities can be delivered using this facility, but the important component will be the required learning outcomes:

- Are the students undertaking this unit to develop skills in a particular activity?

- Will students be focusing on developing a knowledge/ understanding of different tactics, formations or concepts?

- Are students expected to identify strengths/areas for improvement in their own/others' work?

Usually, long-term planning will be organised by an individual in the department, and they will need to take in to account a number of factors. These factors could include:

- Facilities available
- Weather conditions
- Seasonal activities
- Number of groups being taught at one time.

The most common concepts of long-term planning include allocating a facility/area to a member of staff, either termly or half termly. This creates approximately 6 weeks in which to develop our medium-term planning, or 'units of work'.

Medium-term planning

This element of planning refers to the learning outcomes which are expected to be delivered.

It is common that these are generally 'year group' specific, and relatively vague to allow the teacher an opportunity to refine their plans in accordance to their individual class/students.

Medium-term planning needs to take into account what is expected of students by the end of the unit. It comprises of a series of lessons which will need to be planned using this information.

Data such as previous assessments and content covered previously will be very important at this stage of planning to ensure the content being covered is correctly pitched to your students. This will ensure that there is a continuity of learning present, and should form part of a progressive process.

Effective medium-term planning may need to take the following into consideration:

1. **The students being taught**: This could include information such as age, gender and ability.

2. **Previous learning**: Information regarding what content has already been covered, and what activities have been used to reach certain learning outcomes.

3. **Previous assessment data**: Previously this would have been in the form of a National Curriculum level, or information using level descriptors. Every department will have their own methods of assessment, and this information will need to be used to support your planning.

4. **Duration of the unit**: How many lessons will this planning comprise of?

5. **Aim(s)**: What do you plan to teach throughout the unit? What are the expected outcomes for your class?

6. **Content**: This includes any knowledge, skills, or understanding which you plan to use throughout this unit.

7. **Assessment**: This will include how you will be assessing the progress of the students during the unit. This could be in the form of a formal assessment at the end of the unit, or on-going assessments throughout.

8. **Specific information about students**: If students within your class have any individual learning needs – such as a 'Special Educational Need' or communicate using a different language, strategies will need to be planned to cater for these students and ensure they also meet your expected outcomes.

9. **Differentiation strategies**: Considerations need to be made about how students learn to maximise the progress every student can make within your lessons. Therefore, you will need to consider how different concepts can be adapted to meet the needs of your students.

10. **Links to other subjects**: Highlighting potential cross-curricular links can be an important way to maximize the understanding of topics. This could include how the unit can be related to a particular topic within mathematics (such as angles or flight).

11. **Resources**: A list of the equipment that will be required to deliver this unit of work. This could include sport-specific equipment (e.g. appropriate sized footballs), playing area, teaching aids (cones, bibs, markers), technology (such as video cameras)

and sources of information for this unit (useful websites, reference books).

12. **Next steps**: What will this unit progress on to? How will it link to the learning outcomes of the next unit or Key Stage?

In essence, medium-term planning presents a list of content which needs to be covered in each lesson – but taking into account the expected outcomes of the unit as a whole.

Using medium-term planning, you will be able to refine your ideas, and create bespoke lessons for your classes within your short-term planning.

Short-term planning

The previously discussed medium-term planning will form the foundations for your short-term planning, otherwise known as 'lesson plans'.

These will contain more detailed information on how particular learning objectives will be met, including the activities which will form your lesson and any assessment tasks which will be used.

Lesson plans take many forms, and teacher training providers will have their own template to be used throughout the training year. Beyond this, it is important to find a format which works best for you.

Regardless of your decided template, many features of the lesson plan will be consistent. This may contain some of the following features:

Learning objectives

This is the aim(s) of the lesson, and must refer to the content of the medium-term planning.

This can take many forms, but will need to be refined and individualised for your specific class.

One effective method of constructing a lesson's learning objective, is to outline what students will learn as a result of your teaching. This can then be categorised into three types of outcome: all, most, and some.

All: This will outline what all students will learn from your lesson. This element of the learning objective will need to be accessed by all students, and will commonly contain low-order skills such as identifying, demonstrating, selecting and describing.

Most: This outlines the aim for the majority of the students, but extends students from solely retaining knowledge, to being able to perform skills, tactics or concepts. This objective aims to meet the needs of the majority of the class, so will need to be specific to the ability you are teaching. It could contain skills such as explaining, applying and refining.

Some: This learning objective will be aimed at your most-able students. It is important to include this objective to ensure that these students are adequately stretched in your lessons, and continue to make progress at the same rate as the other students. This objective tends to utilise higher-order skills, such as analysis and justification.

Example 1: Gymnastics (types of travel)

All: Students will be able to describe three different methods of travel within an observed gymnastics routine.

Most: Students will be able to perform at least two methods of travel within a short gymnastics routine.

Some: Students will be able to evaluate the movements being performed by themselves, or others, and suggest ways that the performance could be improved.

Example 2: Basketball (developing skills: set shot)

All: Students will be able to describe the key coaching points of the set shot.

Most: Students will be able to demonstrate the set shot with consistency and accuracy in isolation.

Some: Students will be able to perform the set shot within small-sided games while under pressure.

Example 3: Dance (basic choreographic devices)

All: Students will be able to identify and describe the choreographic devices being used in a motif.

Most: Students will be able to apply choreographic devices to a short motif to increase the complexity of the performance.

Some: Students will be able to apply three or more choreographic devices and provide constructive feedback to others to improve their short motif.

Example 4: Fitness (devising a basic circuit training session)

All: Students will be able to identify a range of different activities to form part of their circuit training session.

Most: Students will effectively select different activities specific to their individual training needs.

Some: Students will be able to apply the basic training principle of overload to their planned circuit session.

Lesson episodes

This part of your lesson plan will contain the detail of the activities you plan to deliver at each stage of the lesson.

Your lesson can usually be split into three distinctive sections: starter, main activity/activities, and plenary.

Starter

This part of the lesson can also be known as an introduction, or warm-up.

Your lesson starters will eventually become bespoke to your own teaching style, but is a very important component of your lesson. The starter will 'set the scene' for your lesson, and

Planning essentials

highlight what your expected outcomes will be. This will inform students, and if done effectively, will increase their engagement with the lesson's content.

Effective starters will include the following:

- Recap of previous learning
- Intended learning outcomes.

Within the Physical Education environment, the starter may be planned to take place within the changing rooms. This could be an effective way to encourage group discussions without being negatively affected by the influences of the weather when working outside.

If this is not an option, which can be common – especially when teaching mixed gender groups – it is important to minimise the amount of 'teacher talk' at the start of the lesson. In cold weather environments, standing still listening to the teacher is the easiest way to create a disinterest for the lesson, and may result in behaviour issues.

In relation to health and safety, this section of your lesson will also need to include a warm-up to prepare students adequately for the physical activities which they will be expected to participate in within the lesson.

One effective strategy which is commonly seen within our subject is allowing students to conduct warm-ups independently. Students can be presented with the context of the lesson, and asked to devise their own preparation activities. This will also create an opportunity for you to assess their understanding, prior to the main section of the lesson.

This method does rely on some preparation work with your classes. Making sure that students are aware of what an appropriate warm-up should contain, and having a range of ideas at their disposal will allow students to access this task effectively.

Main activity

This part of you lesson plan will describe the activities you plan to deliver. It is important to ensure that all the tasks you choose to use can be related back to your initial learning objective.

Another important consideration for this phase of the lesson is to ensure that activities are progressive, and develop in the level of challenge to ensure that adequate progress is being made.

Practical example 1: Push pass in hockey

Task 1: In pairs, students are required to demonstrate a push pass, focusing on the key points highlighted during the demonstration of the skill.

Task 2: Students continue to demonstrate the push pass, but under increased difficulty (via increased distance, or smaller target area).

Task 3: Students are required to demonstrate the skill in a dynamic context, creating a more realistic environment to help application of the push pass.

Task 4: Within a small area, students are required to maintain possession of the ball using the push pass while under pressure from a defender. This could be two or three vs one, and can be made more difficult by adding defenders or making the playing area smaller.

Task 5: Apply the push pass within a competitive task, such as small-sided games.

Practical example 2: Development of a short dance motif

Task 1: Replicate short components of a short dance motif.

Task 2: Link components of the motif together to create the motif in its entirety.

Task 3: Modify the motif via the application of a choreographic device*.

* Choreographic device – a method used within dance to develop or vary practical material.

41

Planning essentials

Task 4: Add an additional component to you dance motif.

Task 5: Teach your new component to another group, and learn their additional component and add to your dance motif.

You will need to consider the amount of time available in the lesson in order to plan enough content. Equally, tasks do not need to be progressive as the examples above, you may choose to do a range of different activities which are all linked to the same objective.

The sporting activity you are using to meet your learning objectives will also need to be considered, as this may present opportunities to utilise different methods of presentation, such as a 'whole-part-whole', or 'progressive part' approach.

Plenary

This is your planned end to the lesson, which needs to be used to summarise learning. It could also be known as a summary or conclusion.

This stage of the lesson allows you to review the learning process, which does not need to contribute a significant amount of the lesson time.

Summarising what has been covered in the lesson, reviewing your key teaching points, highlighting key terminology used, and discussing further applications or 'next steps' can all take place in your plenary.

Although this is bound to be 'teacher led', the considerations within the start of the lesson are consistent. You will need to avoid long periods of time where the teacher is just talking at the students.

It is important for this episode of your lesson to be creative. This part of the lesson should be used as an opportunity for students to discuss the learning objectives of the lesson. This could be completed in small groups, or by asking students to demonstrate key teaching points practically and using the rest of the students to evaluate.

It is a worthwhile consideration planning a wide range of creative plenary activities which you can use within your teaching.

Changing time

Although your planning will suggest that your lesson begins with your starter activity or warm-up, it is important to note that it actually begins when students arrive at the changing rooms.

This is another feature unique to our subject which you will need to consider within your planning. Changing time will need to be allocated, which can contribute a significant proportion of your lesson if it is not managed effectively.

Departments you visit may have their own routines and policies for changing rooms, but it is important to acknowledge this is the start of your lesson and should be present within your planning.

Devising creative tasks which students can consider, or discuss while changing can be very effective. An open-ended question on a whiteboard, or a discussion about a sporting performance which occurred recently can engage students for your lesson, while not impacting the timings of your lesson.

Timings

Your lesson plan will also need to show how long each element of your lesson is due to take. This does not need to be rigid, but will ensure that you have sufficient content in your lesson.

As stated above, this will need to include time allocated for the students to change in and out of their PE kits, but will also need to consider the duration of each task.

Managing your time within the lesson will then become much easier – you can plan for more complex and demanding activities to have a larger contribution of the lesson time, while ensuring the pace of your lesson retains the students interest and engagement.

Organisation of students

Another factor which is worth considering in your short-term planning is the organisation of students.

Planning essentials

Unlike within a classroom environment, we do not have tables and seating plans which can be used for the management of students. Therefore, it is important to consider how we arrange students at different stages of the lesson.

You will need to consider each task within your lesson. Then decide whether tasks should be produced individually, in pairs, in small groups or in teams.

Considerations will also need to be made regarding which students work together, this should be completed as part of your planning. The following questions could be used to aid the organisation of groups within your planning:

- What students work most effectively together?
- Are there certain students within the class you would like to separate as part of a behaviour management strategy?
- Would the task be more effective if completed with students of similar abilities?
- Can your groupings be used throughout different phases of the lesson?

It is important to not just rely on students always arranging themselves into groups. This can create situations which can be detrimental to students' confidence and motivation – such as some less-able students always being picked last.

Differentiation

This section of your planning refers to how you plan to adapt elements of your lesson to ensure that all students are making progress (see also Chapter 5: *Effective differentiation within PE*).

This section of your planning will be unique to the class and students you are teaching. But you will need to consider, and plan for the needs of all students:

- Do you have a provision in place for students that speak English as an additional language?

- Can students with a physical disability access the tasks you have planned?
- Do you require any specialist or alternative equipment?
- Will all students be able to complete the planned activities?
- Do the activities stretch and challenge students adequately?

This section of your planning should make reference to these questions, and provide details on how you will cater for specific students if appropriate support is required.

Assessment

Throughout your lesson, you will need to devise ways in which you can assess the students. This assessment does not need to be formal, it may just form part of the learning experience for your students.

Informal assessments of students' knowledge, and checking the progress students are making throughout the lesson is an important feature of any lesson.

This could be in the form of how well a task is being completed, maybe a point score, or the rate of success being achieved. Equally, it could be in the form of some carefully planned questions to check students' understanding of the learning objectives.

Formal assessments could include a short test, or performance which gives students an opportunity to display their work.

All opportunities for assessment, whether formal or informal will need to be planned, and present within the short-term planning.

Key terminology

Another key factor of your planning will be detailing the key terminology which will be used throughout your lesson. Again, this will need to be related to the learning objective, and may be present within the medium-term planning.

Terminology can be present throughout all elements of the lesson, whether it be within your questioning, or key terms you refer to when speaking to the class or individuals.

Ensuring that these terms are present within your lesson plan will help to ensure they remain within the core of the lesson – and compliment the learning objectives.

The vocabulary will need to continue developing throughout the learning journey of the student, so building upon this, recapping and using continuously will help students to understand and apply the terms independently.

Resources

Each element of your lesson, particularly the main tasks, may require significant amounts of equipment. This could vary from a bag of footballs (of the appropriate size) to a range of gymnastics apparatus.

It is important to ensure your short-term planning contains a detailed list of the equipment you require for each lesson. Part of your organisation will then need to include ensuring that this equipment is ready and available to you for your lesson.

These checks will need to include ensuring that: balls are adequately inflated; you have the correct number of items; bibs are correct in number/size/colour, and so on.

Considerations for planning

When discussing planning throughout this chapter, references have been made to the different types of planning, and how they should be used effectively. However, there are a number of additional factors which you should also consider:

Flexibility: Medium and short-term planning should be designed to allow the teacher some level of flexibility.

Teaching needs to be bespoke, and every lesson is different due to a number of factors. Lessons may need to be adapted throughout your teaching in accordance to how students are completing tasks.

Perhaps you are teaching a rugby lesson outside in December, and the weather changes, which creates a much lower temperature – your short-term planning will need to take this into consideration.

Adaptions in short-term planning may impact medium-term planning, this needs to be accepted. But ensuring learning objectives are maintained will ensure no detrimental effects will be produced due to changes to your planning.

Collaboration: The most effective planning takes place in collaboration. Working with your teaching colleagues to produce plans allows for professional conversations, the sharing of ideas and reflections to occur – which will positively influence the work within your department.

This should include sharing resources which can be used by others, or better still, creating resources together as with the short, medium and long-planning.

Continually review your planning: The plans produced will need to be regularly reviewed and adapted throughout the school year.

Teaching is a developing occupation, which needs to be reviewed, refined, and adapted regularly to ensure we are maximising the learning experience for our students. As with planning, doing this in collaboration is most effective, and can be done throughout the school year.

Good practice would also utilise students in this process. Gaining an insight into what students enjoyed, or elements which allowed them to progress at a faster rate is useful information which can be used to inform your future planning and teaching.

Purchased long/medium/short-term planning: Many companies have invested time and resources in producing a number of plans for teaching within PE. These vary in format and content, but can provide good examples, activities and ideas.

Other schools are generally happy to share ideas, planning materials and resources in a similar way – but it is still important to ensure that these are used to inform your planning, and not just be inherited.

Planning essentials

If using any of these provisions, it is important to continue to refine your plans, and ensure you plan for the class and students that you are teaching, and not just delivering a rigid lesson plan.

CHAPTER SUMMARY

- Planning is an essential component of the teaching profession.
- Planning can be divided into three sub-categories: short, medium and long term.
- All elements of planning need to have a constant theme – linked to the expected learning outcomes of your students.
- Learning objectives should be differentiated, as with tasks to ensure that all students can achieve and make progress.
- Short-term planning includes detail to guide you through your lessons (including factors such as groupings, tasks, assessments and resources).
- Planning should not be rigid; it should be designed so that our teaching can be adapted and flexible to enhance the learning experience for our students.

TALKING POINTS

1. What needs to be included within an effective lesson plan?
2. Consider a learning objective within one of your lessons, can you modify the objective to ensure that all students within your class can achieve within the lesson?
3. How much detail should be included within medium and long-term planning?
4. What methods can you use within your planning to ensure your teaching remains flexible and adaptable?

4 Assessment essentials

Assessment has become an essential component of teaching any subject, but a practical subject such as PE has many implications which will need to be considered early on in your teaching career.

First: What is assessment? And why is it important for our subject?

Assessment, in its most basic form, can be referred to as any measurement(s) that are obtained within our teaching. This can come in many forms such as test scores within an examination course, or a student answering a question verbally on the tennis court.

This topic can be divided into two key areas of assessment:

1. **Assessment for Learning**: This refers to assessments that help students to learn more effectively.

    Example: A teacher asking questions during a task.

2. **Assessment of Learning**: Assessments which are made to measure learning and progress formally.

    Example: A written test at the end of a unit of work.

So why do we need assessment within Physical Education? Surely the health outcomes which derive from the subject could be argued to be more purposeful for our students than measuring knowledge and skill development?

Assessment essentials

In relation to whole-school data, assessment is very important. This data provides vast amounts of information which can be used within, and outside of, the PE department. This includes:

- Measurements of attainment of all students, within all subjects
- Highlights educational improvements/outcomes
- Gauges the effectiveness of a school, or department
- Increases accountability of teachers.

When highlighting the positive outcomes of assessment within PE, similar benefits can be described. However, the key benefit is improving the students' learning experience. This could include:

- Measuring outcomes of a task, or unit of work
- Highlighting strengths and areas for improvement
- Underlining the progress of a student or class
- Informing our planning to ensure our lessons are adequately cater for the needs of our students
- Adding to department reflections: Are units of work, or individual lessons effective?
- Increasing motivation and enthusiasm for students.

Presenting information regarding where a student is currently at in relation to knowledge, understanding or performance is important, but more so will be the professional conversations that derive from this. Explaining how or what students need to do to improve is a valuable part of teaching and learning – and is one of the things which sets us apart from sports coaches.

Assessment will differ depending on the context PE is being taught. For example, assessment within core Physical Education, following the National Curriculum for PE will be different compared to a GCSE PE assessment.

For examination courses, assessment advice and guidance can be found with particular examination boards and providers – but the same themes of assessment can be discussed generally.

So, what are the types of assessment? And how can they be implemented within PE?

Assessment for Learning

As defined earlier in this chapter, this form of assessment refers to any assessments which are used within our teaching that influences the learning experience for our students.

This can also be known as formative assessments, or the acronym 'AFL'. The following are types of Assessment for Learning, with some examples applied from a PE context.

1. **Self-assessments**: This refers to engaging students in a reflective process to assess themselves following the completion of a task.

This could make use of some set criteria, or learning outcomes, which students will need to refer to in order to increase the accuracy of their judgements.

Example 1: Dance performance: Students have been asked to develop a short dance motif over a series of lessons. By videoing their performance, the students can review their own work, and suggest ways their performance could be improved.

This could also include a checklist to guide students towards ensuring their motifs include the relevant content expected, linked to the learning objectives of the lesson or unit of work.

Example 2: Tactics/strategies in athletics: After performing a 400m race, students are asked to reflect on their performance.

What were the strengths of their race? Did the student have an effective start to the race which allowed them to dictate their own pace? Or did they apply a strong finish to the race – showing an acceleration throughout the last 200m? Could any tactics be changed, or applied to their race in an attempt to improve their 400m time in future events?

These tactics/strategies could be conducted via a score out of ten, a star rating (out of five stars), or could be in the form of a written or verbal comment.

Again, this will need to be linked to the learning objectives of the lesson, but should inform any future performances/assessments within this activity area.

2. **Peer assessments**: This is a similar process to self-assessments, but relies on students reflecting on the work of others. This form of assessment can be more effective compared to the above due to it engaging students in developmental conversations, which has a positive impact on the learning for all students involved.

The format of these tasks will also be consistent with self-assessments; a set criteria will be needed for students to refer to, and these will need to be linked to the expected outcomes of the lesson.

Example 1: Bowling in cricket: The learning objective of this lesson is to improve 'line and length' of bowling.

Students complete a bowling over, with a partner marking where each of their bowls are 'pitched' on the cricket strip by placing a cone or marker, where the ball hits the ground. Following the completion of their bowling over, reflections can be made regarding the effectiveness of their bowling, and assessing the 'line and length' of their bowls.

These reflections could be in written form, but this would need careful consideration as you would not want to lose the enthusiasm of the group.

Instead, verbal comments, or a simple score rating would be more effective. Ensuring the students are appropriately evaluating their work, while maintaining a purposeful pace to the task.

This could be progressed to explaining which bowl was most, or least effective, or providing strategies to improve their bowling.

Example 2: Floor routine in gymnastics: Students are asked to observe their peers performing their routines. Using agreed criteria prior to the observation, students can reflect on the work of others and suggest strategies to improve their work.

Questions such as 'what worked well?' and 'what would improve this performance?' will guide students to make appropriate responses.

An effective way for students to do this would be within a group discussion. This would allow students to discuss their work, and possible improvements.

Students may require some guidance from you, possibly in the form of some starting questions, or some additional questions or prompts to help them elaborate on their points/suggestions.

For example: 'Name one component of the floor routine which you liked' leading to 'Explain to the performer what it was that made this component a strength of their routine'.

Younger students may prefer teaching strategies such as 'two stars and a wish', which asks students to provide two strengths of the performance, and suggest one strategy for students to improve their work.

3. **Target-setting**: This form of assessment relies on the students being able to effectively reflect on their own work, and highlight the outcomes they wish to produce.

This could be implemented before a task is undertaken, or at the end of a task if the students will have an opportunity to improve their work.

As with 'goal setting' in sport, the targets produced by the students will need to meet the following 'SMART' criteria:

- **Specific**: Define the target, and include as much detail as possible. For example: Who is going to achieve it? What are they going to do? And why are they doing it in the first place?
- **Measurable**: How will targets be monitored? How will their progress be tracked?
- **Attainable**: Is the goal actually achievable for the student? This is an important factor to ensure the target is not 'out of reach' for the student, and therefore affect their motivation.

- **Relevant**: Is the target relevant to the lesson objectives? And will it be an effective way of improving the students work?

- **Timely**: What is the time-frame for this target? Is it to be achieved by the end of the lesson? Or a series of lessons?

Example: Basketball lay-ups: At the start of a basketball unit of work, students are asked to produce a personal target to improve their lay-up skill.

Pupils will be required to construct a target using the above 'SMART' target guidelines and could include: 'To be able to score 10 lay-ups in a row with my non-dominant hand', or 'To score more points from lay-ups within games'.

These targets alone are not useful for the students, as they are too vague, not meeting the requirements of the first of the 'SMART' target guidelines.

Students will therefore need to be guided through this process, allowing them to self-reflect, and devise methods to reach their own expected outcomes.

4. **Questioning**: As previously mentioned within Chapter 5: *Effective differentiation within Physical Education*, this method of assessment can give a teacher instant knowledge of a students' understanding of a task or topic.

Questions need to be thoroughly planned and thought-through to ensure they are pitched at an appropriate level, but can be used as a very effective form of assessment.

The structure of the questions will need to coincide with the tiered approach of Bloom's Taxonomy (discussed in Chapter 5), and include opportunities for the students to extend their answers via open-ended questions.

It will be common that students respond to your questions with short, closed responses. You will need to continually follow-up these responses with further questions, probing their knowledge to gauge their understanding.

This will allow the teacher, and the student, an opportunity to judge the level of understanding the student possesses, while also providing an insight into what the student needs to learn to progress further.

Example: Please refer to Chapter 5: *Effective differentiation within PE*, for an applied example of tiered questioning within a football passing context.

5. **Shared learning outcome(s)**: Expected learning outcomes of a unit of work tend to be relatively rigid within teaching (as discussed in Chapter 2: *Curriculum essentials in Physical Education*).

But what about if we were to involve the students in devising the learning objectives for individual lessons?

This process would enable students to reflect on their current levels of skill/knowledge/understanding, and highlight potential targets for them to progress towards.

This form of assessment needs to include group/class discussions, and relies on students having a good understanding of the activity they are currently learning.

Example: Serving in tennis: Students are asked at the start of the lesson to decide on an objective for the lesson, related to the skill highlighted to be developed, in this case the tennis serve.

Less-able students may highlight that they currently lack consistency within this skill in isolation, and may produce a learning outcome to include some basic technical knowledge which could be applied to simple tasks.

For example, improving their ball-toss in isolation to ensure they are producing adequate height of the tennis ball to effectively serve over the net.

More-able students may choose to devise a more complex learning objective, which could include strategies and tactics within serving, such as applying top-spin to serves, or directing serves into specific areas of the service box.

By allowing students to be included in the construction of the learning objective, the teacher will be able to guide the class to effectively reflect on their own ability within the topic, and appropriately highlight ways in which they can progress within the lesson.

Assessment of Learning

This form of assessment, as defined earlier within this chapter, includes more formal judgements being made on the work of the students within your class.

For these assessments to be effective, they must be directly influenced by the objectives of the lesson, or unit of work. They must also be reliable and consistent measurements to ensure all students are assessed in the same way.

Within a classroom environment, this type of assessment is simple. Written pieces of work that are formally submitted, and given a grade or mark for example. This could also be in the form of short tests, or formal examinations.

But how does Assessment of Learning occur within the practical environments within PE?

The same fundamental characteristics are consistent; the assessments are directly influenced by the expected outcomes, and the assessments need to be consistent for all students to ensure effective judgements are made about their progress.

For example, if the objective of a cricket unit of work is to develop basic 'sport-specific' skills, then the formal assessments made will need to be related to a range of basic skills within the activity, such as throwing, catching, fielding skills, bowling, batting, etc.

This could be achieved by a range of skill related activities, which allow students to perform the required skills – while also providing an opportunity for the teacher to assess their work/ performance.

In order to make an accurate, and formal Assessment of Learning, you will need to have the following skills:

1. **An ability to critically analyse practical skills**: This highlights the need of the teacher to appropriately highlight parts of a skill which are not technically correct, and suggest strategies for the student to address these to improve their performance. This will need to be within isolated skills practices and competitive environments.

2. **Sufficient subject knowledge**: Sport-specific knowledge will be essential to be able to analyse certain elements of an activity, and provide knowledge for the students to improve their work. It is not expected that a PE teacher is an expert in all activity areas, but you will be expected to have an appropriate and effective level of knowledge to ensure students can meet the agreed learning outcomes of the unit of work being taught.

3. **Be able to identify an appropriate success criteria**: You will be required to have an understanding of the steps that students will need to take to meet the expected learning outcomes of a unit of work. You will therefore need to construct appropriate success criteria relevant to the outcomes of the activity being taught. It is also important that students are able to understand the criteria to ensure they are able to meet the expected outcomes.

4. **Be able to make effective judgements based on the success criteria**: Once the appropriate success criteria have been produced and agreed, you will then need to be able to make official judgements based on this. These will need to be accurate to ensure all students know exactly where they are at, in relation to their learning, and more importantly, what they need to do to improve.

Without the above skills and abilities, you will be unable to make effective assessments of learning.

When producing assessments of a practical skill, it may be useful to break the skill down into smaller sections in order to make effective judgements.

Example: Backward roll in gymnastics

Table 4.1 Example of assessment proforma to aid the assessment of a backward roll in gymnastics

Pupil	Lower body towards ground with body close to the heels	Chin remains on the chest (back rounded)	Hands flat on ground with their thumbs close to ears	Strong arm movement pushing body to upright position	Feet down first and use momentum to move to standing position
A	✓	✓	✓	✓	✓
B	✓	✗	✓	✓	✓
C	✓	✓	✓	✗	✗
D	✓	✓	✓	✓	✗

This structure would allow you to highlight specific components of a skill to formally assess the student's performance of a backward roll. The assessment data within Table 4.1 suggests the following:

Pupil A: Is able to perform the skill effectively, with evidence of all of the expected learning outcomes highlighted within the lesson.

Pupil B: Preparation for the skill is effective, but an incorrect head position causes their back to not be shaped in an effective position to perform the skill efficiently.

Pupil C: Preparation and execution of the backward roll is effective, but the student may lack upper body strength to move into the upright position. Lack of momentum may also be the cause of this fault.

Pupil D: All elements of the skill are evident, but the pupil lacks speed and confidence to gain the appropriate amount of momentum to finish the skill effectively.

This type of proforma is very simple to produce, and can allow you to effectively ensure that assessments take into account all of the expected outcomes expected.

It is important early on in your teaching career that you keep a written/formal record of the assessments of learning that you make within your lessons. These will be important when you come to producing formal reports, or planning for future lessons with this class.

Assessments of learning do not need to take place just at the end of a unit of work, but can also take place to measure progress throughout a unit, or be used to inform your planning. This will allow you to use the information to ensure your lessons adequately challenge your class, and build upon their previous learning.

National Curriculum of PE assessments

Previously, it was expected that students were given formal assessments using 'grade descriptors' as part of the National Curriculum for Physical Education (NCPE).

To allow teachers to do this, attainment targets were written which highlighted expected learning outcomes within key processes, such as 'Development of Skills'. Students were then given a level from 1 to 8, with an exceptional performance level above this for students that were achieving beyond the expected outcomes.

The most recent NCPE reforms (2014) have developed this further by removing the level system, and empowering teachers to assess students within outcomes specific to their own classes. This is called 'assessment without levels'.

Departments are now required to design their own assessment protocols to allow schools to assess in accordance to the needs of their own students. This usually takes the form of students being categorised within units of work, and could take the following form:

Example of assessment categories
(Year 7 – skill development)

- **Basic**: The student displays an ability to perform basic skills in isolation, but lack consistency and accuracy.

- **Adequate**: The student is able to perform basic skills in isolation consistently/accurately, but their performance decreases when applying to more challenging tasks.

- **Secure**: The student is able to perform skills within isolation and within more challenging tasks. Consistency and accuracy decreases when the student is put under pressure.

- **Advanced**: The student is effectively able to apply skills to isolated and challenging tasks. This includes application to competitive situations.

- **Excelling**: The student is able to appropriately apply skills to competitive tasks/full versions of the activity with accuracy, confidence and flair.

This style of Assessment of Learning allows departments to devise their own success criteria for their students. These categories are not restrictive, and differ from school-to-school.

However, the key characteristics highlighted earlier are still important; assessments must be linked to the learning outcomes of the unit of work, and assessments must be consistent.

Assessments within examination courses

These assessments differ between different examination providers, but core themes still exist.

It is important to ensure that these assessments are accurate and recorded formally as they are likely to form part of the controlled assessment component of a course.

Controlled assessments refer to any assessments made which contribute to a student's final grade within the subject. These assessments will need to be submitted to the examination provider, as you would do with coursework.

For GCSE Physical Education, the most recent reform (2017) requires students to be assessed in three practical activities (one must be from and team and individual sport).

These usually require the teacher to assess a student's performance in practical activities and give two numerative marks: one mark for their ability to perform specific and predetermined skills in isolation, and another mark for their performance during a competitive version of the activity.

These assessments are submitted to the examination board towards the end of the final year of study, and they will arrange a moderation or assessment visit to ensure your marks/assessments are accurate.

Examination boards have different assessment frameworks for teachers to use, such as levels, but you will need to familiarise yourself with the assessment protocols unique to the examination board that your department chooses to use.

There are also a number of vocational courses within Physical Education that use alternative methods of assessment. This includes BTEC diploma courses, and Sports Leadership Awards.

These are usually evidence-based assessments, and support materials can be accessed from the course provider.

Consistency of assessments

One of the most significant flaws since Physical Education has included formal assessments has been the consistency of the assessments.

Assessments which take place in different schools, or by different teachers, or that take place at different times in the academic year can be affected by so many variables which make the assessments very difficult to be consistent.

Assessment essentials

It is important that these variables are reduced as much as possible within a department, so that planning, comparisons and progress data is accurate within your school – and there are a number of ways this can be done:

1. **Collaboration**: Assessments for learning that are made with more than one member of teaching staff. Not only will this produce more accurate assessments, but it will also provide a platform for staff to have professional conversations regarding assessment which will also have a positive effect.

2. **Moderation**: It is not always possible to get a number of staff available at one time to produce assessments. However, moderating assessments can overcome this.

   This method acts more as a quality assurance process, rather than an assessment – and will require you to make your assessment(s) prior to the moderation process.

   Possibly video recording some tasks within your lesson, and using a department meeting to collaboratively assess the students can be very effective.

   This could also take the form of students being invited from a number of different classes to do a live assessment activity. This is similar to those undertaken in many GCSE practical assessments.

3. **Core tasks**: Classes perform pre-agreed assessment tasks, which are consistent across different teaching groups. With this process, all students will be assessed performing the same task, increasing the accuracy of assessments between classes.

   An important consideration of this method will be ensuring that the task can be accessed by all students. Allowing students with a basic level of performance to be assessed alongside those students who may be excelling.

Reporting

The department you work in will have its own policy on what data or assessments need reporting.

Data in schools refers to any information available about an individual student, or class. These can range from reading scores, to formal test scores, such as SATs assessment levels.

This reporting could just be part of tracking department progress, or could be information which is communicated with others, such as parents or form tutors.

It is important that you are aware of when this formal reporting takes place, and the methods in which you are required to complete it.

It is becoming more common that schools make use of online reporting systems, which are usually web-based. The advantage of these systems is that the reporting can become accessible to everyone instantly.

If parents and students are able to access formal assessment data independently, they should be able to use this to increase their learning experience. Parents/guardians will also be able to oversee their progress and give additional support where necessary.

One of the most important features of reporting however, is ensuring the information is understood. Numbers/grades alone make sense to a trained/qualified individual, but for this information to be useful to students and parents may need some additional information.

Additional data, such as teacher predictions and target grades are also important to highlight how the student is attaining in relation to their current progress and their ability.

Alternative assessment methods

This chapter so far has explored a number of assessment methods linked to Physical Education. But it is important to note that there are some additional processes and outcomes which are important to our subject.

Assessments which make reference to students' attitudes and behaviour are also important – particularly when reporting to parents/guardians.

Within secondary Physical Education, it is not uncommon to have students within our classes that lack fundamental physical skills, or have poor physical literacy. Therefore, assessments such as 'effort' can be an important reporting tool.

Some schools now make use of termly assessments which report effort and behaviour together, sometimes known as an 'attitude to learning', and students can be categorised appropriately using statements like the following:

- **Exemplary**: The student displays an outstanding level of effort and behaviour within lessons.

- **Good**: The student displays good levels of behaviour and effort, and completes all work to the best of their ability.

- **Coasting**: The student at times completes work, but not to the best of their ability.

- **Disengaged**: The student sometimes completes work set, but lacks effort.

- **Disruptive**: The student shows poor levels of effort and behaviour, and tends to affect the learning of others.

Other data which may be useful within Physical Education could include basic fitness information.

It is not uncommon for PE departments to include Fitness units-of-work, which could easily include a small battery of fitness tests. This would provide a greater range of physical assessments.

These fitness assessments would need to be re-administered throughout the student's educational journey to show the progress students are making in relation to their physical fitness.

CHAPTER SUMMARY

- Assessment refers to measuring the knowledge and outcomes of our students.
- Assessment can be divided into two categories: Assessment for Learning and Assessment of Learning.
- Assessments form an important part of whole-school data, but is also an important tool for a teaching which should inform planning.
- Any forms of assessment must be linked to the expected learning outcomes of the lesson, or unit of work.
- Summative assessments must be accurate and consistent.
- You will need to consider the best methods of assessment, and ensure you conform with your department/school assessment policy.
- If you are assessing as part of an examination course (such as GCSE PE), make sure you are familiar with the assessment criteria available from the specific examination board.

TALKING POINTS

1. How can you ensure that assessments you make are accurate and consistent?
2. How can you use previous assessments of students to inform your planning?
3. If you were to use target setting as a self-assessment tool, how can you ensure your students produce effective and meaningful targets?
4. When do you feel that your summative assessments should be completed?

5 Effective differentiation within PE

Within the classes we teach, every student present will be unique. These distinctive characteristics need to be identified to ensure that the lesson can be adapted for their needs and give every student the opportunity to learn.

This process can be labelled in numerous ways, such as 'mixed-ability teaching', 'personalisation' or 'individualisation'. Differentiation is a current 'buzz word' in education – but what does it mean for us as PE teachers?

The term refers to a teacher's ability to modify the learning experience for students, based upon their learning needs. This is one of the most important elements for us as PE teachers, and sets us apart from non-education specialists, such as sports coaches and instructors.

Differentiation can take many forms, and needs to cater for all students in your classes, regardless of their position on the ability spectrum. This may be in relation to stretching our most-able students, or providing less-able students with additional support to ensure they can still access your learning objectives.

The forms of differentiation can be divided into these three categories:

- Task
- Process
- Outcome.

Within each category, and number of provisions can be used to provide students with an effective, but personal learning experience.

Differentiation by task

This category refers to how we can adapt the tasks we present to students within our lessons. Within the practical environment, a number of strategies can be considered, and with effective planning, can optimize the learning experience for our students.

1. **Groupings**: Throughout practical lessons, particularly when teaching invasion games, a number of tasks can be developed to encourage students working collaboratively. Groupings can be considered to modify the way in which students learn, and there are a number of approaches this can be used:

- *Mixed-ability groupings*: This is where students within each group share a number of different abilities, which can range from the least-able student to the most able in each class.

   This approach to grouping can present increased opportunities for reciprocal learning. More-able students can be used in a capacity to support the less-able individuals, which in itself can provide adequate challenge for all the students within the task.

   This strategy may also increase the rate of progress of your less-able students as they may feel more comfortable to seek advice/support from fellow peers rather than yourself as their teacher.

   It is important to consider, however, the frequency that this approach is used. Overusing your most-able students in a 'coaching' capacity will have significant positive effects on their social and inter-personal ability, but will eventually lead to detrimental effects on their progress within their practical ability.

When teaching invasion games which provide opportunities for students to work in teams, this approach is also effective when organizing teams.

Mixed-ability groupings will usually provide an even competition between other groups within the class, and provide a smooth transition from activities to small-sided games.

However, great care needs to be taken when considering the difficulty of the task you apply to the group. There is usually a tendency for less-experienced teachers to pitch tasks to the 'average' ability students, which therefore will have negative effects on the progress made by the students at the extremities of the ability spectrum.

- *Similar-ability groupings*: This refers to students being grouped with other students of a similar ability.

  This approach is particularly useful when working with your most-able students. The tasks that these students can be asked to complete will allow them to operate at a higher level and extend their boundaries. Expectations of this group will usually be much higher when compared to their less-able peers within the class.

  These groups can often be more capable of completing tasks more independently. This will include students providing each other with feedback.

  For your less-able students, this method of grouping presents an opportunity for you to provide additional support.

  The tasks that they are asked to complete may be pitched at a lower level initially to allow them to access the content of the lesson, or may be used to increase confidence before the difficulty of the task is increased.

2. **Pacing/timing (acceleration)**: Your most-able individuals will more often than not, progress through a series of activities at a much faster rate than their less-able peers.

During tasks, it can be appropriate to devise extension tasks which can be completed by students which progress faster than the rest of the class. These tasks will also need to be relevant to the lesson objectives, but can provide students an opportunity to develop a deeper understanding of the lesson content.

For example, if you have asked your class to complete a simple lay-up drill during a basketball lesson and you see a number of students are able to complete the task at ease, there are a number of tasks which can be applied.

Observation and analysis tasks involving their peers can be very easily applied, which will develop an increased understanding of the lay-up skill. Or the students can be asked to apply the skill to a more competitive situation to develop an understanding of when the skill can be applied to the full-version of the sport.

However, great care will need to be taken, as it can be seen negatively by some students that are being given more work as a result of the tasks they are being asked to complete being too easy.

Another key consideration which needs to be monitored when increasing your pace of delivery is ensuring that a lack in the depth of understanding does not occur. Accelerated pace can sometimes not allow students to deepen their understanding of topics, and can at times be detrimental to the development of higher order thinking skills.

3. **Roles**: The majority of tasks that are presented to students within lessons can be undertaken in different ways. Students can be presented with a problem, and left to consider an effective way to solve it.

Within practical lessons, a number of roles can be allocated to develop different levels of understanding, and at times, develop different skills. These include:

- Coach
- Official
- Choreographer
- Leader
- Participant (positions/tactics).

4. **Space**: A key consideration of most practical lessons is the physical environment you choose. When out on the school field, this can be a unique opportunity to modify tasks.

Usually, the space we choose to use a dictated by a number of variables, such as time, weather or other classes potentially sharing the facility. But how often do you consider the space in which you give students in order to complete tasks?

For example, when teaching a games lesson, if the size of the space a group of students are working within decreases, the pressure that the student will be under will increase to perform a skill/movement – therefore increasing the difficulty of the given task.

Consider a basic possession task within a games activity. If you were to apply a '3 vs 1' task, the space that groups are working in can change in accordance to their ability, or even during the task is being completed.

If students are struggling to maintain possession, and are seen to be making mistakes due to the pressure of the defender, then increasing the space will increase their rate of success. Your more-able students can be subjected to the opposite (reduction in space) which will increase the difficulty of the task. This will require them to perform skills faster, and react to their opposition more quickly.

This strategy could also be used by the students themselves. Allowing your students to modify the space they complete the task independently will act as an excellent self-assessment of their ability to complete the task.

Differentiation by process

This category refers to the various ways we can adapt our lessons in order for the students to complete tasks. This can include how tasks are completed, how work is presented to students or resources which can be used by the students to meet the desired outcomes.

1. **Resources/materials**: This is a very effective method of differentiation for Physical Education. It can be very easily applied to tasks, and can be modified as students become more competent within any given task.

Changing the equipment being used by the students can increase, or decrease the difficulty of tasks – this is dependent on the activity being taught.

Let's consider a basic tennis lesson. A number of resources can be modified to increase/decrease task difficulty:

- *Tennis rackets*: The use of short-handled rackets will decrease the difficulty of a task. This is an effective way to teach basic skills to students which have had very little experience of the sport, or those that may be lacking the appropriate hand-eye co-ordination ability.

- *Tennis balls*: These can come in various varieties. Short tennis balls (foam-like material) are good for beginners/young students. These move relatively slowly, and are effective when developing very basic co-ordination, to moving towards basic strokes (e.g. the forehand).

  Regular tennis balls also differ, low-density balls can be used which ensure a low bounce height and slower ball speed – allowing the students more time to play good tennis shots and increasing the amount of success during tasks.

  This then progresses on to standard balls, which move faster, and bounce higher – therefore increasing the difficulty of the task. These are appropriate for students that have mastered the basic skills, and are beginning to play the full-version of the sport on full-sized courts.

- *Nets/courts*: Once again, the playing area can be adapted to suit the needs of our students. To start with, it is worth considering if a net is even needed. Some strokes, or co-ordination tasks can be more effective without using a net – this is an effective way to increase confidence before progressing to versions of game-play.

The height of nets can also vary dependent on ability. Short-tennis nets are slightly lower than conventional nets, thus making tasks easier at the earlier stages of skill development.

Court sizes must also be considered. When playing with low-density balls, the court size must be altered as they will not travel as far as the standard ball.

Mini-tennis court sizes are very similar to standard badminton courts; this is a good starting point which will progress to full tennis courts as their ability increases.

2. **Support**: The input that is given to students during tasks can also present a good way to differentiate tasks. Our more-able students should be stretched by being set problems which they need to attempt to solve independently.

Newly-qualified teachers tend to 'over-teach' and present students with support throughout all stages of the lesson. However, in order for these students to be challenged, it is important to present them with opportunities to improve their work without large volumes of teacher input.

They may be able to solve these problems independently, or in collaboration with other students. It is important to ensure that teacher input is only given when really necessary – this will increase their independence, while also having a positive effect on resilience and dealing with tasks that are not accomplished so easily.

The less-able students may not have the required skills to work as autonomously, therefore, it will be appropriate to provide these students with more teacher-support during tasks.

This could be in the form of additional demonstrations, verbal feedback, or mechanical guidance. It may even be appropriate to modify the task as earlier explained in this chapter.

3. **Teaching style**: The way in which we teach will have a massive impact upon the students in our classes. Most lessons within our subject will require a range of teaching styles being adopted, in order to cater for all groups of students.

A large number of educational researchers have investigated the different ways in which students learn, and how our teaching style can influence learning – these are just a sample of the styles we can employ to improve the learning experience within PE:

- *Command style*: This is the most basic style of teaching, and most appropriate when working with less-able students, or with students that have very limited experience of the task/activity they are being taught.

  This style is very didactic, and involves students responding to the commands of the teacher. This includes what, where, when and how. All decisions being made are by the teacher.

  Application: This can be a very effective method when teaching our more 'dangerous' activities, and is common in unit of work within athletics, for example, when teaching javelin or shot put.

  Within this context, students will generally be positioned in lines, ordered when to throw/collect the apparatus, and often demonstrated the appropriate method to use.

  Equally, this can be a very effective way to support our less-able students in a variety of contexts. For example, it may be appropriate to use this style when teaching a 'set shot' in basketball, or an 'instep pass' in football. If a student lacks the confidence, and knowledge, to effectively perform a skill – this method can be very effective to isolate the teaching points and make rapid progress.

- *Reciprocal style:* This is another well-used style within PE. It requires our students to evaluate the work of others.

  This style will need some prescribed criteria to begin with to ensure the feedback being given throughout the task is relevant. As the student's knowledge increases, the volume/ detail of the criteria can decrease as students should be able to determine their own success criteria using their prior knowledge.

This method does however rely on students having a high-level of social skills in order to communicate effectively with their peers during the tasks.

It is important to ensure appropriate terminology is used when using this style. For example, students should be asked to 'identify strengths and areas for improvement', rather than 'strengths and weaknesses' to ensure confidence of students is not damaged by peers giving feedback.

Application: During a basketball lesson, you are teaching the fundamentals of a 'set shot'. Students can be paired up, one performing the task, the other observing the task being completed.

The observer can be focusing on the criteria agreed upon by the lesson objectives: How the hold the ball, the placement of the performer's feet (stance), the movement of the dominant arm during the shot (follow-through), and the trajectory of the ball flight.

At a more basic level, the observer could just track the success rate of the performer. For example, how many successful set shots are scored, how many are attempted and then calculating the percentage of success.

- *Guided discovery*: This style can also be known as 'problem solving'. This entails the teacher presenting the students with a question/problem, and students are required to answer/solve it.

  This style will require students to work more independently, but the level of teacher-input can be related to the student's ability/skill set. This will require a certain amount of prior learning, depending on the difficulty of the task.

  Pupils with high levels of creativity will often flourish in this environment as it presents opportunities for them to trial ideas, and adapt technique and skills as they see appropriate.

<u>Application</u>: This can be very effective when teaching tactics and strategies, or tasks which may have a number of different methods of completion.

For example, during a basketball lesson, you could ask the students to devise a number of 'set-plays' to employ into small-sided games.

The students will be able to be creative as there are infinite ways this task can be completed – but it will require a certain amount of prior learning: for example, how to outwit an opponent, screening, rules associated, etc.

4. **Questioning**: PE teachers are stereotypically very good at this element of teaching. This stems from our experience teaching within practical contexts, where a large volume of our assessments are made from students' verbal responses.

As with teaching styles, a large volume of research has been done investigating the effective use of questioning by teachers – the most used information being derived from 'Bloom's Taxonomy of Questioning'.

'Bloom's Taxonomy' sets out a series of 'levels' in which questions can be constructed using differing levels of challenge:

a. *Knowledge*: Observation and recall of information. Using terms such as list, define, describe and identify are good examples of this level of questioning.

    <u>Example</u>: 'What part of the foot is used during an instep pass?'

b. *Comprehension*: This tier requires the student to under-stand information. This can include interpreting facts, or comparing/contrasting pieces of information.

    <u>Example</u>: 'Predict where the ball will end up if the per-former over-rotates at the hip during a kicking action in football?'

c. *Application*: This level involves the student using information. This level of questioning is often associated with the guided discovery teaching style referred to earlier in this chapter.

> Example: 'When in a game of football would this pass be appropriate?'

d. *Analysis*: This type of questioning can be very useful within reciprocal learning tasks. It requires the pupils to identify key components of the task, or recognize key factors which may influence performance.

> Example: 'Compare your partner's passing technique to the "perfect model" – select and explain the differences in the techniques.'

e. *Synthesis*: Students will need to draw upon knowledge from several sources in order to respond effectively. This can include predictions and drawing basic conclusions.

> Example: 'Formulate a method to create an activity to improve your partner's passing technique.'

f. *Evaluation*: This is referred to as the top-level of questioning. These should be pitched at your most-able students, and will require a large volume of understanding/prior knowledge to access.

> This can include answering using different/contrasting information, or making decisions based on gathered evidence.

> Example: 'Recommend a training method which will improve your partner's short-range passing.'

To ensure our most-able students are challenged in relation to questioning, it is important to present opportunities for them to elaborate on their responses. This will help you to gauge their level of understanding.

Open-ended questions are essential when trying to understand the process in which responses are given. This may be in the form of additional probing following a response, for example using 'why' as a precursor to a question.

5. **ICT**: Technology is constantly developing, as is its presence within education.

A number of modern resources can be used to help us to differentiate during PE lessons. A good example of this is video analysis.

Although video analysis has been present for many years, the way in which it can be used has developed significantly. The introduction of analysis software, such as 'Coach's Eye', allows students to critically analyse performances.

Slow-motion playback, identifying joint angles, and highlighting particular parts of the body during a skill can be very effective forms of guidance for students which may be struggling with the performance of a skill.

Similarly, allowing your more-able students to use this technology independently can aid reciprocal learning, and deepen their understanding of why particular errors may be occurring during a performance.

In addition to this, the ability to playback video sources within a practical environment is now very common, and forms part of our students' everyday life.

This enables our students to compare their technique to that of a professional athlete. This serves well to deepen technical understanding of a performance, and allows them to identify fine adjustments to improve their work.

Differentiation by outcome

This category refers to how we adapt the result of a task or activity depending on the student's ability. The objective of the lesson remains the same, however, the outcome of the task may differ depending on the understanding the student possesses.

Great care is needed when using this form of differentiation as it can be de-motivating for our less-able students. When used inappropriately, it can cause students to feel that they are 'no good' or formally categorised as 'bottom of the class'. This can obviously have very detrimental effects on confidence and progress.

Therefore, planning tasks effectively – ensuring that the final outcome is constantly referred to will be important. Regular feedback during the tasks, and re-visiting the lessons' learning objectives is essential to maintain the students interest and justifying way they are completing the given tasks.

The easiest method to employ this is devising a number of tasks which achieve a similar outcome. This must contain a number of activities that progress in difficulty, ensuring that students complete the tasks that are pitched at the right level of challenge.

Application: Let's consider a lesson focusing on a short forehand serve in badminton. A number of different tasks can be put into place, focusing on the same objective – development of this skill.

1. **Basic technique drill**: Students are to perform a forehand serve which aims to land the shuttle in the correct service box.

2. **Refining the skill**: Students are to perform the short forehand serve aiming for a target positioned close to the service line (starting with a hoop, and decreasing target size as success increases). In this exercise, the skill is the same, but the focus is now on refining the technique, developing accuracy and consistency.

3. **Further refinement**: Students are to perform the short forehand serve, aiming for cones placed in both corners of the service box, close to the service line. This exercise again builds upon prior knowledge of the skill, but now requires the students to modify their technique to aim their serve to different targets. The variety of serve will aid them when applying the skill into game situations.

Further to this, task outcome can also be related to the learning needs of our students. In PE, this could take the form of dialogue, demonstrations, group discussions, verbal feedback or analysis of performance.

For any of the differentiation strategies to be effective, it is essential that you know the students well. Prior to teaching the class at the early stages of a school year – information such a CAT scores (Cognitive Assessment Tests) can be useful to start to identify the type of learner you are catering for.

As you start to get to know your classes better, you will be able to employ different strategies to ensure you maximise their learning experience.

CHAPTER SUMMARY

- Differentiation refers to a teacher's ability to modify the learning experience for students, based upon their learning needs.
- It can be applied in three ways: task, process and outcome.
- Differentiation by task refers to how we can adapt the tasks we present to students within our lessons.
- Differentiation by process refers to the various ways we can adapt our lessons in order for the students to complete tasks.
- Differentiation by outcome refers to how we adapt the result of a task or activity depending on the student's ability.
- All forms of differentiation require the teacher to understand the best ways in which our students learn, and how best to cater for their needs.

TALKING POINTS

1. Consider a topic you are currently teaching. Using Bloom's Taxonomy of Questioning, create a number of questions which differ in difficulty.
2. When is an appropriate time to pose these questions to your students?
3. What ways can you adapt a simple drill? Consider supporting your less-able students, while also challenging your most-able.
4. How can you make use of ICT within your lessons? And how can you ensure this can be accessible to all of your students?

6 Providing for the most able within PE

Before considering the range of provision for this distinctive group of students, we should define what it is that makes students 'Able, Gifted and Talented' in Physical Education.

Our most-able students can be labelled in a variety of ways depending on your school, such as:

- High achieving students (HAPs)
- Able, Gifted and Talented (AG&T), or
- Most able and committed.

Whatever term they may be labelled, the characteristics they possess remain the same.

Identification of these students is also dependent on the school you work in. Here are some suggestions that you could use to recognise your most-able students:

1. **Teacher nominations**: Teachers (previous and/or current) can select students they deem to be high ability.

2. **Parent/peer/student nominations**: Other people within the process could identify gifted/talented students. This includes students being able to nominate themselves.

3. **Existing assessment data**: Using whatever assessment protocols are within your department to identify those that are attaining the highest.

4. **Sport surveys**: Auditing sport participation inside and outside of school.

5. **Fitness/skill testing**: Using a battery of small-scale tests (e.g. Illinois Agility Test, Harvard Step Test, problem-solving tasks) to identify students.

The identification process you use must be well thought through and thorough. The following four principles are useful when planning your own talent identification system: transparent, fair, rigorous and regularly reviewed.

Students classified in this group will exhibit high ability in one or a combination of the following five areas:

1. **Physical**: This can be skill or fitness related, but often refers to high level performance. At an early age, it can be related to fundamental skills (such as speed or agility).

2. **Creative**: Problem solving and critical thinking. Students who show high levels of innovation, or flair, when outwitting opponents or choreographing performances.

3. **Cognitive**: Students display high levels of knowledge and understanding. They can usually articulate answers using advanced terminology, and perform well particularly within theoretical tasks.

4. **Personal**: The learner will display high levels of motivation, sets goals independently and shows commitment/resilience to difficult tasks.

5. **Social**: Pupils that demonstrate excellent leadership skills such as communication and confidence. These students work well within groups/teams.

Using these five areas can inform how we approach the provisions we offer. But what happens within our lessons if these students are not catered for?

If our most-able students are not stretched by the tasks we provide, lessons will become tedious and behaviour issues may appear. More importantly, the progress that these students display will decline.

Many different provisions can be employed to cater for our high-achieving students. These can be divided into provisions within, and outside of lessons:

Within lessons:

● High-order questioning

● Advanced techniques and tactics

● Variety of roles

● Extension tasks.

Outside of lessons:

● School sport competition pathway

● Junior Athlete Education Programme (JAE)

● Multi-skills academy

● Additional qualifications.

Within lessons

Higher-order questioning

Questioning our most-able students is more than a formative method of assessment. It also provides an opportunity for students to elaborate on initial responses, or allows the student to focus on the process of their answer, rather than just the end product.

At a basic level, it is important to ensure that as many openended questions are used. These allow the students an opportunity to expand their responses, and give justification or explanation for their answers.

For example, in a basketball lesson with a focus on tactics, your lesson objective is to understand and apply different tactics of defensive play. A question you may ask a student could be:

Providing for the most able within PE

'What defensive strategy did that team play?' This question will only allow a closed-response, and will not encourage the student to explain the thought-process or justify their answer.

Instead, framing the question to allow the student to elaborate on their answer will stretch the individual, and therefore deepen their understanding: 'Why did this team decide to use the defensive tactic they did?' or 'What was effective about the defensive tactic used?'

Bloom's Taxonomy of Questioning suggests that questions can be classified into levels, and the questions that a student can access depend on their learning ability and understanding.

In relation to this model, the top three levels of questioning can be used to describe more appropriate questions to be pitched to your more-able students: analysis, synthesis and lastly, evaluation.

To explain these three-tiers of questioning, we can use a typical football lesson focused on short-distance passing. With the aim of our questions stretching the gifted students beyond just recalling information.

Analysis refers to breaking an answer, or concept, down into smaller components – which in turn should create an increased understanding. For example: 'Watch your partner passing the ball, what is happening to their technique which causes the ball to move towards the player's left side?'

Synthesis is where the student is required to solve a problem, integrating knowledge from a range of sources. It is usually the case that this level cannot be used until the previous level of questioning (analysis) has been completed.

For example: 'Now you have identified the cause(s) of the ball tending to move towards the performer's left side, devise a practice that will improve the accuracy of their pass.'

The last level, *evaluation*, requires the student to make judgments based on their ideas/prior knowledge. However, these questions also need to include an explanation and justification of their response.

For example: 'What would be the most effective way to improve the accuracy of their pass, and why do you think this will be effective?'

Advanced techniques and tactics

This provision is activity-specific, but it is important to consider the content of your lessons to ensure you stretch talented individuals where possible. It does, however, rely on good subject knowledge, and access to demonstrations (or resources if this is not possible).

It may be possible to differentiate your lesson by task. Providing your more-able students to develop more complex skills, while other students within the class are developing a more basic skill, but with the same focus.

For example, in a badminton lesson with a focus on the overhead clear, the majority of the class are refining the skill in isolation. Your most able students can effectively perform the skill, so you decide to make the task more challenging. These students are now required to start at the net, and move towards the back of the court to perform the clear, or possibly feeding the shuttle to their weaker side to develop their footwork associated with the same skill.

The same principle can be used for tactics. You may have some students in your class that need to focus on basic tactics, such as man-to-man defensive in basketball. However, a group of your more-able students can start to use more complex tactics such as screening, or zonal defence.

Both tasks can still be undertaken at the same time, while working towards the same lesson objective. However, the task will need to be pitched appropriately to ensure the students are adequately challenged.

Variety of roles

Making use of alternative roles can also be an effective way of challenging students in different ways. These can be as an evaluator, coach, leader, manager, official or choreographer.

For example, if you are teaching volleyball to a group of Year 8 students, and one of your class is a national-level performer – the content of a typical scheme-of-work would not challenge this student at all.

Allowing this student to lead a variety of tasks, which they select in relation to the lesson objective, can be an effective way of stretching the pupil. They are now presented with a problem, and are required to develop a solution.

Additionally, the student could be used in the capacity of a coach. Providing peers with critical feedback to help their development of a skill, while improving their own analysis ability. Suggesting ways to improve technique will need to be incorporated, but will require the student having sound knowledge of the skill being taught.

The role of the coach can also be taken a step further within competitive situations. The student may be presented with a team to develop in particular scenarios. Their role will now require them to assess the game, and make decisions based on this information, while ensuring other team members are aware of their own roles.

Care needs to be taken, however, to ensure that certain roles are not overused. It may be that a talented performer that can perform skills consistently well may feel uncomfortable, or ineffective at coaching their peers.

Extension tasks

More often than not, our most-able students will progress through tasks at a faster rate in comparison to their peers. Therefore, it is important to consider the difficulty and content necessary to challenge them.

Extension tasks refer to additional tasks that will take students a step further in their learning. These are an effective way of ensuring that students do not become bored within lessons, and also allow students to deepen their knowledge, while completing the essential work at the centre of the lesson.

Care must be taken with extension tasks, as it is not always a popular decision with students to be rewarded for completing their work with additional tasks. However, within practical lessons, extension tasks can be provided very subtlety.

To put this into context, consider teaching an overhead serve in tennis. The task you have presented the class is to perform the skill in isolation, and record how many serves the students manage to perform effectively.

A group of more-able students can perform this task with success, therefore suggesting the task is not challenging enough. The extension task they can be presented with is now directing their serve towards smaller targets within the service box.

Therefore, this progression to the original task subtlety changes the difficulty of the work being completed, while ensuring the students are appropriately challenged.

Outside of lessons

The role of a PE teacher goes beyond the classroom on many occasions. One of these is the role we play in developing talent outside of the taught curriculum. Extra-curricular opportunities provide an opportunity for PE teachers to develop talent creatively, and a number of these provisions will be outlined below.

School sport competition pathway

This pathway refers to the movement of students from being introduced to a sport/activity within a PE lesson, and progressing to performing at an elite level.

Providing for the most able within PE

The most problematic stage of this process is the movement from school to a sports club, mainly due to the number of people that may be involved; directors of sport, heads of PE, PE teachers, primary link teachers, external coaches, or non-specialist teachers/volunteers can be part of a school's extra-curricular provision. For the system to be effective, all involved will need to understand how the pathway works.

A simplified way to describe the pathway can be described from Physical Education to national/international teams or events:

1. **Physical Education**: Students are taught fundamental skills, and are then introduced to a broad range of activities.

2. **Intra-school sport**: Students are presented with an opportunity to apply taught skills in a competitive environment within their own school.

3. **Inter-school sport**: Students further develop their skills in a competitive environment against students from other schools.

4. **Community sports club**: Students' progress to a club/team outside of school. A sport-specific coach will usually be present to provide expertise.

5. **Regional/county squads/events**: Access to more challenging competitions. Expert/experienced coaches will be used.

6. **National/international squads/events**: Elite level competitions. Professional coaching and support staff.

Part of our role as PE teachers is to know where/who to direct our talented students towards. National Governing Bodies (NGBs) and County Sports Partnerships (CSPs) will be useful resources for you to access this information.

There are a number of strategies, however, that will have very little impact. Posters around school, and word-of-mouth can be no substitute for an individual approach which involves you guiding and supporting the student towards appropriate provisions.

The most effective pathways perform when all partners work in collaboration. For example, using community sports club coaches to support school provisions. Arranging taster sessions within your curriculum PE lessons led by coaches from local clubs can be a powerful tool to encourage your talented students to join community teams in their own time.

Junior Athlete Education Programme (JAE)

This is a programme coordinated by the Youth Sport Trust (YST) and was formally implemented by Specialist Sports Colleges. This aims at developing talented sports students via a range of support materials.

The programme is designed to be bespoke and can be tailored around your students' needs. Typical models consist of workshops (sometimes led by athlete mentors), information to engage/involve parents/guardians, and resources for the students to use themselves.

The support students will be given include:

- Performance improvement
- Goal setting
- Time management
- Diet support
- Communication.

The most effective examples of JAE are within PE departments that have used the resources to develop their own support system. Getting all of your talented sports students together regularly provides an opportunity for you to develop a range of generic skills that can help them in sport, and in life.

Additional support that you can offer these students could include:

- Individual mentoring (by PE teachers, or older sports students)
- Strength and conditioning
- Flexibility

- Psychological preparation
- Medium/long term planning
- Financial support
- Characteristics of a role model.

When planning a provision for your students involving some of the topics above, it is important to ensure that whomever delivers the content has sound subject knowledge within the topic. Using community sports coaches, teachers from other subjects, or professional athletes can provide you with the expertise needed to develop a success programme.

Multi-skills academy

A danger of the provision above can be that young students tend to narrow their skill set upon one sporting activity too early. This can have detrimental effects on students maintaining motivation later on in their school/sporting careers, but can also negatively impact their progress in other activity areas within PE.

Therefore, a multi-skills approach can be more beneficial, particularly with younger students that you teach.

The first element of this provision is to encourage the students to reflect on their current skill sets and abilities. This can be done using generic components of fitness or life-skills that your academy aims to develop. This could include agility, strength, flexibility or self-confidence.

Using sports that are unfamiliar to the students will be very powerful, and will ensure that their skill development is not too focused on their main activity. For example, using judo can have positive effects on a number of activities.

Judo will help develop the students' core strength which can be attributed to a very wide number of sports. Not to mention developing other generic components such as flexibility, strength, co-ordination and muscular endurance. More importantly though, activities like this will aid the development of some inter-personal skills, which could include:

- Resilience
- Confidence
- Sportsmanship
- Spatial awareness
- Etiquette.

Additional qualifications

Many organisations have produced PE and sport-specific qualifications and courses which can be used to further develop our gifted and talented students.

Sports Leaders UK is a popular organisation within schools which provides qualifications which can be accessed by students that can demonstrate a good understanding of leadership.

The level 1 and 2 qualifications are very straight forward, and resources are readily available for you to access. Both of these require the students to complete a series of modules, which can be assessed by you verbally, in writing or by observation within a practical context. Modules include:

- Developing leadership skills
- Plan, lead and evaluate sports sessions
- Assist in planning/leading a sports event.

There are some age constraints and total qualification time requirements that need to be adhered to, but regular courses and support are available from the Sports Leaders UK.

To run a course, you must also be accredited as a centre and complete their tutor training, but this presents a great inset opportunity for any PE teacher that has not been through this process before.

Providing for the most able within PE

Young people that display particular strengths within activities may also benefit from sport-specific qualifications. Sports Coach UK is responsible for standardising the qualifications across all NGBs and Level 1 coaching awards are designed to give people basic coaching skills within a chosen sport.

Most level 1 awards are focused on generic coaching skills, developing basic coaching principles so that the student can support coaching sessions effectively.

These principles include communication skills, and how to engage people in physical activity associated with the sport. Basic skill develop activities are usually presented, giving the student an increased subject knowledge of how to coach sport-specific skills.

The qualifications range from level 1 to 4, progressing in difficulty. Within schools, students will very rarely progress beyond level 2, mainly due to age requirements to access the award. However, the cost of some awards can be substantial, and may require students to fund courses themselves.

Officiating awards can also be very useful, particularly in departments which encourage students to contribute to the school's extra-curricular provision.

Contacting the NGB for specific sports can give more information about particular awards, however, some organisations provide good entry-level qualifications. Introductions to officiating and non-official qualifications can sometimes be more beneficial.

These qualifications will not allow the students to officiate full versions of their sport, but will develop their skills as an official, and should allow them to contribute to intra/inter-school competitions.

For example, teaching students how to table-judge a basketball fixture can have many advantages. For the student, this creates an opportunity to develop sport-specific knowledge, as well as increasing their understanding of the roles and responsibilities of an official during a basketball match. For the PE teacher, this will present an opportunity for students to support any school sport fixtures.

CHAPTER SUMMARY

- Establish what is meant by 'Gifted and Talented' within your department.
- Develop a system for identifying these students which is transparent, fair, rigorous and continuously reviewed.
- Ensure you cater for high-ability students within, and outside of lessons.
- Be sure to think creatively, and create a bespoke programme of support/develop for your sporting talent.

TALKING POINTS

1. What characteristics do you think a 'Gifted and Talented' student in PE would possess?
2. How can you identify these students within your lessons?
3. What ways can you ensure that your most-able students are stretched within your lessons? Particularly if they are currently learning an activity which is a strength to them.
4. In what ways could you support talented sports students outside of their PE lessons?

7

Providing for students with special education needs within PE

Within your classes there will be some students that require additional levels of support to make progress at the same rate as other students, or to just access the tasks being presented to them.

This is an important consideration for you as a teacher to ensure that your lessons are inclusive for all students, and that you adhere to every students' right to an inclusive education.

Every individual student will need a personal approach which is bespoke to them, but there are some suggestions which can help you prepare to teach students with additional needs.

But how can you cater for every student individually within a class? And more importantly within the practical environment of PE?

Firstly, you will need to know the group you are teaching. Prior to teaching a class, schools will have a wealth of information regarding each student – this will include any special educational need they may require. Be sure to ask for this information prior to planning your lesson.

Secondly, you will need to understand what special educational needs are, and how to best cater for students with these needs.

Below are some of the most common educational needs that tend to have an impact on Physical Education, with a brief definition of each need, and some practical examples of how you can provide support within your lessons:

94

1. **Physical disabilities**: Students with any physical disability may require support within practical lessons, such as specialist equipment or modified tasks.

It is important to understand exactly what the disability is in order to plan appropriately.

It is worth your time researching any disabilities which students may have had diagnosed within your classes to get a full understanding prior to teaching.

For example, it is common for students to have conditions that affect the strength of bones (osteoporosis). Some students may have a severe case of this condition, meaning they will be unable to participate in contact/high impact activities.

On the other hand, they may have minor cases which may just require some alternative provisions, such as not playing full-contact versions of the sport.

Physical disabilities also include temporary disabilities, such as broken limbs. More details on this educational need will be detailed later in this chapter.

Practical suggestion 1: Adapted equipment.

Some disabilities may not allow students to use standard sports equipment. One of the easiest applications of this is the size of the ball which is used in any given activity.

For example, consider teaching a rounders lesson with a student who is partially sighted. Using a bigger ball, which is brightly coloured may allow this student to access the activity.

This provision is also useful for students who may lack the basic co-ordination skills required by this activity.

In this example, it may also be appropriate to allow the student to wear a catching glove, or mitt, to help their ability to catch the ball within competitive activities.

Practical suggestion 2: Modified tasks/rules.

It is important to ensure that all of the students within your class can access the learning objectives of your lesson. However, how they meet these objectives can be different.

95

Students with special education needs

Adapting rules within certain activities may allow students with physical disabilities to still develop sport-specific skills via modified activities.

Consider teaching a net/wall activity such as tennis. Lowering the net height, or making the court smaller may allow students to start to apply developed skills within adapted, but still competitive environments.

2.   **English as an additional language (EAL):** This refers to any students that speak English as their second language.

It is a reasonably vague term, as it does not present any information regarding their understanding of the English language.

This is important information to discover prior to your teaching as you need to be sure they can understand your instructions in order to keep your lesson safe.

There are a number of strategies you can employ to support students in this situation, while also developing their use/understanding of the English language.

Practical suggestion 1: Translated instructions.

Creating resources which have some basic instructions translated into the students first language may be an appropriate strategy, particularly if there is important safety information which you need them to understand.

It is important that these resources are not too detailed, but it may be useful to include some diagrams or images to help increase their understanding of a task.

Practical suggestion 2: Basic language and key terminology.

After your explanation has been delivered to the class, you will need to discover whether your instructions have been fully understood.

Planning a more simplified set of instructions, using basic language, and slower delivery of the information will help the student to understand your instructions verbally.

Although it is important to use basic and simple language in order to increase their understanding, it is still important to use key terminology.

This key terminology may need to be explained, or re-framed, but it is an important part of their learning to understand and use these terms independently.

Practical suggestion 3: Pairing with other students.

Students who speak English as a second language tend to lack confidence in speaking tasks, or contributing to group discussions. By pairing students with EAL, with other students within your class, you will automatically be creating a safe environment for them to communicate.

Furthermore, by selecting the paired student carefully, such as socially confident individuals, this method will be more effective.

Try to include them in dialogue where possible in smaller groups, help them frame their responses to your questions, and apply terminology.

3. **Behavioural issues**: This refers to any issues which may be present within your class regarding behaviour.

In a practical environment, it is important that these students are highlighted to ensure you keep your lessons safe.

Usually, any behavioural issues are categorised as low, moderate and high – which will give you a little bit more information regarding your potential strategies.

The most important consideration in managing the behaviour of students, is providing clear and consistent expectations of students (more information on behaviour is present in Chapter 9: *Ensuring good behaviour in PE lessons*).

It may be that any behaviour issues are due to medical conditions, such as 'Attention deficit disorder' (ADD) or 'Attention deficit/ hyperactivity disorder' (ADHD). If this is the case, this will be highlighted on the student's information.

Students with special education needs

When teaching students with ADD, ADHD or any other behavioural concern, there are a number of methods you can put into place to avoid challenging behaviour.

Below are some simple examples you can apply to your planning:

- **Presenting information in small steps**: Try to not overload a student with too much information at once.

   By offering instructions in small, bite-sized chunks, they will find it easier to get a full understanding of the task.

   One of the main causes of students losing focus during a task is due to confusion, or not fully understanding instructions, so if this can be reduced it should decrease the probability of these students disengaging.

- **Active involvement of the student**: Try to involve the student in instructions.

   This could be done by asking simple questions throughout instructions, or asking the student to repeat an instruction to keep their focus, such as:

   'Can you repeat that last point for me please?'

   'Where do you think would be the best position for the groups to set up our next task?'

   This will also have the added effect of maintaining the focus of other students, as they will now be conscious they may be asked to repeat some information, or answer a question directed to them.

   Another example of this is to use the student in the management of equipment. Setting up drills via placing cones or markers, collecting in balls after a task, or having additional responsibilities may maintain their focus.

   It is important not to overuse this method to ensure it does not have the opposite effect and decrease motivation – they may start to feel unfairly treated.

- **Short-term goals**: By producing small, short-term goals, students will experience success more often. This will cause an increase in motivation, and an increase in confidence.

Students with special education needs

Tasks like this could begin in the changing room: 'Let's see if you can get changed today in under four minutes.'

Throughout tasks, small goals, or targets could be created for students who may lack motivation or focus – such as more process related goals:

'How many passes can you do within one minute?'

'Once you have completed ten passes, try increasing the distance you are passing by one more metre.'

- **Short tasks**: Produce tasks which maintain a high pace within your lesson. Tasks which continue for a long period of time, or that are too repetitive could lead to students getting bored and losing focus.

  This could be avoided by preparing tasks which can be easily adapted, making them more challenging, or adding variety easily.

  Consider a basic set-shot task in basketball. Just taking shots from a free-throw line would get tedious very quickly. But by adding some challenges, changing the shooting location, or adding a rebounder could easily modify the activity to maintain focus.

- **Simple/precise information**: As with the first suggestion, it is important to not overload students with your instructions.

  Consider the language you choose to use to avoid any misunderstandings, and therefore maintain the pace of your lesson.

  For example, in a rugby lesson, you could give the instruction: 'Find a space with your partner for the next activity', this could lead to students going anywhere within your teaching space.

  Instead, consider using language such as 'Find a space, with your partner, which one of you standing on the try-line'.

Students with special education needs

- **Praise**: Providing students with positive feedback throughout tasks will always increase motivation and self-confidence.

  Ensuring students with behavioural issues are regularly praised for good work will keep them on task.

  It is also effective to try to give this from different areas of your teaching space. This will add the effect of reminding them you can still monitor their work without being in close proximity.

  With this method, it is very important that it is used in moderation. By overusing praise, it will lose its desired effect and will no longer be an effective strategy.

- **Increase success**: As with short-term goals, ensuring the students are able to access successes will maintain their engagement in a task.

  Designing tasks which allow students to easily track their progress can be an effective way of achieving this.

  For example, within a badminton lesson, if you were to place a hoop in the area of the court you want the students to direct the shuttlecock, the students will be able to easily see their progress and motivate them to continue with the task to increase their success rate.

  It is also important to ensure that the tasks created are also not too easy, as this will have the opposite effect and create boredom for the students.

- **Frequent feedback/reminders**: Similar to praise, by maintaining a level of verbal communication throughout a task you will ensure the student remains on task.

  Regular feedback will also avoid tasks becoming too difficult, which is another cause for students becoming disinterested.

  Feedback can be positive or negative, as long as it remains related to the objectives of the task.

  In relation to reminders, this could be in the form of regular updates on their expected progress by the end of the task:

'There's only a couple of minutes left to complete this task.'

'Remember the key points I want to apply when performing this skill.'

These can be used to re-focus individuals, and linking the reminders to the learning objectives will be an effective way of applying this.

4. **Health issues**: It may be that there are students within your class that have certain medical conditions related to their health. It is important to have an awareness of these, particularly if they can affect their ability to exercise.

This could include health issues such as Asthma or Hayfever, which although are commonly controlled effectively by students independently, can affect their ability to exercise.

Highlighting these students within your planning is important. This can act as a prompt for you to ensure they bring inhalers with them to the lesson.

More importantly, this information may cause you to alter expectations of strenuous physical tasks, such as long-distance running or fitness tests.

Allergies are also important to note, particularly if you are taking students off-site for a sports activity or fixture.

Knowledge of what they are allergic to is very important if any first aid needs to be administered by you, or a nominated first-aider.

5. **Temporary disabilities**: As mentioned earlier in this chapter, this refers to any physical disabilities which may be short-term, such as broken limbs or concussion.

You will still be required to include these students within your lesson, but this will require some additional planning.

When students have injuries such as broken wrists, which are contained within a plaster-support, it is obvious that the student may not be able to participate practically.

Students with special education needs

This does not mean they cannot still access the learning objectives of the lesson. Could they be used in an alternative role, such as coaching other students linked to the learning objectives?

Creating tasks for these students to still be involved are very important – they must still be involved within your lesson.

Where possible, try to always ensure the student gets changed into their PE kit. This will reinforce to the student that they are still required to participate in the lesson in some form.

This may not be possible for some injuries, but important to maintain if possible.

It is also important to ensure that students only get involved in practical tasks if their health allows them to.

For example, if a student has recently suffered a head injury (like concussion) and been told not to take part in physical activity for two weeks, you must adhere to this information.

Adapting your teaching for disadvantaged students

Although this is not classified as a special educational need, there is still a requirement for the teacher to ensure that all students can access their education – this includes students from disadvantaged backgrounds.

Within schools, students can be known within a group called 'Pupil Premium'. This was a fund which started in 2011 which allocates schools additional funding to support students from disadvantaged backgrounds.

But how does this affect their participation within PE?

Students that are coming from low-income families may struggle to purchase the required equipment needed for PE.

This could include studded boots for activities such as football or rugby.

If situations like this occur within your teaching, speak to a member of staff who oversees pastoral support as there may be funding available to support this student.

In relation to our role as a teacher, being aware of the students within your classes that fall within this category is important.

It may be that you need to relax certain uniform policies, such as sanctions in place for forgotten equipment/kit.

It is also important to note who these students are to ensure that they make the same amount of progress as all of the other students within your lesson.

CHAPTER SUMMARY

- Every student within your class has a right to inclusive education.
- You are required to adapt your lessons to support students' individual needs.
- Know your class – obtain all of the information you require to plan an effective and inclusive lesson.
- These needs will need to be bespoke – knowledge of their specific needs is essential for you to plan appropriately.
- Including in your planning ways in which tasks or activities can be adapted.
- Ensure that any modifications are still linked to your lesson's learning objectives.
- Every student must be involved in the learning process of your lesson.

Students with special education needs

TALKING POINTS

1. What prior information would be useful to you regarding each student in your class before you beginning your planning?
2. How could you adapt a practical activity by using alternative equipment to support any students with special educational needs?
3. What ways may a student from a disadvantaged background require your support?
4. Should your expectations of any student with an additional learning need be different compared to other students within the class?

8 Use of ICT in Physical Education

The use of Information and Communication Technology (ICT) is ever evolving within education – and recent advances in technology can significantly improve the learning experience of students within PE.

As part of the wider responsibilities of a teacher, it is important that we teach our students how to use ICT effectively within PE. This could include:

- Researching topics using a variety of online sources
- Using a range of ICT tools effectively, and developing transferable skills
- Connect and share ideas, concepts and performances
- Review their own or others' work.

It must also be noted that ICT should not be used to the detriment of physical activity. It is important to ensure that ICT is not used as a 'bolt-on' to your usual practice, and it should be embedded into the culture of your lessons.

We must also ensure that the use of technology does not cause any distractions when teaching in a practical environment. This would be to the detriment of learning/behaviour management, and may result in health and safety concerns.

In this chapter, I will outline how ICT can be used within PE using the following themes:

- Communication (connect/share)
- Analysis (statistics)
- Resources (online/wearable/equipment)
- Assessment (tracking)
- Non-participants.

Communication

This theme refers to students (and teachers) ability to learn, connect and share via the use of technology.

Recent advances in technology have allowed people to communicate through a variety of online systems, such as blogging, social media applications and video streaming sites – but how can these be used to improve the provision in PE?

Blogging: Online blogging can be a safe, and effective platform for students to share ideas, and seek the support of others independently. This could include pupils uploading drills, ideas they have planned for lessons or revision resources to aid others.

Example: Creating a blogging platform for a group of sports leaders. This would allow students to discuss their planning ideas when working within small groups outside of curriculum lessons – with you having an oversight of their discussions.

This could include students sharing session plans, reviewing previous leadership tasks, and seeking advice from their peers when appropriate.

This can also be an effective way to allow students from different classes/groups to collaborate – increasing the opportunities for students to work more independently, and review their own/others' work continuously.

Social media applications: Modern mobile phones, tablets and laptops have a wide variety of social media platforms – and when used appropriately can be very effective within PE and school sport.

To ensure that you are protecting yourself online, it is important that you seek advice from your school's ICT team, and make yourself aware of your school's ICT policy.

Creating school groups, pages and discussion forums are very effective, and at times can improve communication, particularly in large schools.

Example: Creation of a Facebook group for a school sports team. Notices can be posted and received by students instantly, reducing the frustration of notes being lost, information not being given, etc.

Team lists can be posted directly to the group, fixture schedules, training/practice discussions (such as tactics), reviewing performances and notices can be distributed on a short time-scale. For example, changing the time of a training session, or reminders to bring in certain pieces of equipment.

For this to be effective, it may be appropriate to create your own 'usage agreement' to ensure students use the discussion platform appropriately.

This also creates an opportunity for the students to take ownership of the provision, and improve communication links between you and your sports team.

Video streaming: This refers to sites which allow students to upload/download videos, which can assist their learning.

Once again, it is important that you seek advice of your ICT support team, and ensure you understand your school's ICT policy if you want students to upload their performances online.

Sites, such as YouTube, are rich with ideas, drills, practices and information which can be used by both students and teachers.

Use of ICT in Physical Education

Instructional videos can be found to allow students to independently plan ways in which they can improve their own work. Informative content can also be found to support academic courses/topics, which can be particularly useful for revision purposes.

Example 1: Using videos to analyse performance: Compare your technique in a sport to the performance of an elite athlete. Students can use online video resources to compare their technique of a skill, to that of a professional performer.

This creates an opportunity for students to reflect on their own work, and critically analyse their performance – allowing them to refine/improve their own technique(s).

Example 2: Uploading a video for feedback: There may be students within your classes that perform at a high-level outside of school. It may be appropriate for the student to upload some of their performance footage to an online platform for you as the teacher to see.

This is incredibly useful if a student wishes to be assessed in an activity not available within your school for an examination course.

This could include activities that require specialist equipment or environments such as skiing or windsurfing.

For this to be effective, the student will require information regarding all of the content they will need to record. Is there a list of pre-determined skills they need to have evidence of? Does the footage need to include footage of them within a competitive environment?

Communicating with the wider school community: Another factor of communication which is worth investigating in relation to technology is how you promote and celebrate PE and school sport with a wider audience.

Social media pages can be created to allow students, families, governors, staff and community partners to hear about things that are happening within your department, such as:

- Upcoming fixtures
- Results
- Sports events/festivals
- Celebrating sporting success stories
- Interesting lesson ideas
- Team photos.

Analysis

The next theme makes reference to ways in which students can critically analyse their own/others' work via the use of ICT.

Digital cameras and performance analysis applications are very useful tools which provide students support when trying to refine their work, and improve their performances.

Digital cameras: Mobile phones, tablets or video cameras allow students to capture performances and instantly review their work. This can be a useful resource for any activity undertaken within PE.

Pausing performances to analyse body positions, or reviewing a groups timing can be very easily seen from the video of the students work – but care must be taken to ensure students remain on task.

This can be done by ensuring students have a particular focus when using the video equipment, such as the inclusion of a brief mini-plenary within the task to allow students to discuss their findings and suggests ways to improve their work.

Care must be taken when using video recording equipment, and you should ensure you know which students have parental permissions to be filmed/photographed.

These issues can be minimised by deleting any footage captured within a lesson following it being reviewed by yourself and the students that have been recorded.

Example: Students record themselves performing a small dance, or gymnastics motif.

This task will require a particular focus, such as reviewing any particular body shapes or movements, or possibly focusing on specific choreographic devices such as cannon and unison. This would also need to be in-line with your lesson objectives and outcomes required within your unit-of-work you are delivering.

Immediately after the performance, students review their work and suggest strategies to refine and develop their work.

Performance analysis applications: There are a number of resources available to support students' ability to analyse their performances using technology.

Previously, it was common for schools to invest in licensed systems such as 'Dartfish' or 'De-ja Vu'. These still remain very effective, but are relatively expensive when compared to more modern (and free) analysis software which is readily available.

There are a number of applications available on smartphones and tablets, which can be very effective within PE.

Applications such as 'Coach's Eye' allows students to easily record a piece of work, and then critically analyse the performance via a number of means:

- Slow-motion replay
- Review visually, frame-by-frame
- Play alongside other performances (students can compare each other's work)
- Obtain angles at joints
- Add lines to suggest ways angles of joints can be refined to improve performance
- Add labels/annotations.

Example: Students work within small groups, with one device per group, using a pre-determined analysis application.

If this was used within a badminton lesson, students may be asked to complete a drill, focused on the 'overhead clear'. Students then use the application to view the execution of the skill and analyse the performance.

Focus could be on:

- The point of impact with the shuttlecock

- The trajectory of the shuttle

- Angle of the elbow joint throughout the skill.

Students could compare each other's performances and highlight the factors which make the skills more, or less, effective.

Resources

This theme will highlight a number of ICT resources which can be used to improve teaching within PE.

Resources can come in many forms, but this section will investigate resources that are available online, technology which is wearable, and some examples of equipment which can support learning.

Online resources: As already discussed, there is a wide variety of online video libraries which can be both easily accessible and very useful.

Sites such as 'YouTube' have a variety of videos which can be very good to improve our subject knowledge. This can present us with new coaching ideas, or drills and practices which can further develop students within our lessons.

There is also a wide variety of websites which are full of subject specific knowledge – such as TeachPE.com.

Topics such as anatomy, physiology, psychology, nutrition and coaching are just a few that can be accessed through such online resources.

These websites provide an additional resource for students to engage with Physical Education independently. This could be to improve their understanding of a topic, deepen their knowledge, or form part of their revision.

Wearable technology: Technology such as heart rate monitors have been readily available for many years, but still have a place within PE.

Teaching students how to use these pieces of equipment is important to ensure students leave school with this skill, which can be applied to their own exercise regimes.

Heart rate monitors allow students to access data instantly regarding the intensity they are exercising at, and can be used as a measurement to indicate their health.

This could include recording heart rates before and after activities, and measuring the time it takes to recover to their resting levels.

Students can then use this knowledge to prepare for certain activities, or design/implement their own training plans.

This technology has recently advanced somewhat, to include more expensive pieces of equipment, such as Fitbits.

Equipment like this can obtain vast amounts of information, such as pedometers, pace, distances, blood pressure, etc. This then provides an opportunity for cross-curricular links in relation to analysing the data.

Example: During a health and fitness lesson, students record their heart rates at specific intervals (for example, every 2 minutes) during a 20-minute continuous training session.

Students then use this data to plot a graph, and analyse what is happening throughout the training session. This could include identifying:

- What happens to heart rate during a warm up?
- How long does it take their heart rate to return to their resting level?
- What percentage of their maximum heart rate do they work during the training? (Link to training zones.)
- Are there any anomalies with the data?

Equipment: A wide range of technology is available through different pieces of equipment.

One of the main issues with most of these is how much some of them cost, but here are a few examples of things that can be effective at relatively small expenditure.

1. *Speed guns*: Allow students to measure how fast objects travel. This can include throwing a cricket ball, or kicking a football.

2. *Flip-cams*: Small video recording devices with a playback screen. These can store limited footage, but provide instant feedback during tasks.

3. *Bluetooth speakers*: Can be used in dance, gymnastics and fitness contexts, and allow audio playback from portable devices (such as smartphones). With a small number of these, students can work in 'break-out' spaces to develop work using different music sources.

4. *Wireless mirroring*: Systems which can be put into place to mirror performances on to a bigger screen to aid the review/ analysis of a task. This would then allow a larger number of students to review a performance at the same time.

5. *Smartphones/tablets*: Allowing students to use their own devices and access applications which contribute to learning (Coach's Eye, Hudl Technique, Runtastic, Myfitnesspal, etc.)

6. *GPS systems*: Accurate methods of obtaining data such as distances travelled, pace, direction, etc. This could be used as an application on a smartphone/device.

Assessment

This theme has a particular focus for us as the teacher, and assessment is one of our key priorities.

ICT can be used in a number of ways to support the assessment of students in PE, track their progress and provide students/parents with information to help them understand how they can improve.

Video recording core assessment tasks: Via the use of video recording, collaborative assessment opportunities can be made within your department.

Not only will this provide a platform for professional conversations with your colleagues, but it will also improve the accuracy of assessment across different groups, and between different members of staff.

Tracking progress: Having an online platform to track the progress of students will prove very useful.

This could be as simple as a spreadsheet where staff record assessments electronically throughout the academic year. This data can then be used at points of the year to inform summative assessments, such as report writing or discussions with parents.

Online assessment/reporting: There is now a number of online resources which can be used in a similar way to track student progress.

Web resources such as 'Go4Schools' and 'Class Do-jo' can be used to allow students, parents and staff instant feedback on assessments which have been recorded online.

These systems do require a license fee, and tend to need engagement across the school. Although, more recent web resources, such as 'Skills2Achieve' have been developed and are subject specific, and endorsed by the Youth Sport Trust.

Non-participants

It is not uncommon for a small number of students to not be able to access some tasks due to the practical nature of our subject (such as due to injury/illness).

It is imperative to ensure that these students are still involved in the learning process of the lesson, and ICT can support this in a number of ways.

Video analysis: Allowing these students to use one of the video analysis methods discussed earlier in this chapter, would be an effective way to engage non-participants within your lessons.

The student can be tasked with collecting video footage and presenting it to the group, while contributing to the analysis discussion.

Collecting data: During competitive tasks, students can be tasked with collecting data. This can include a number of ICT resources, and can be as simple as keeping score, to recording statistics during a game.

Example: During a basketball lesson, the non-participant could be recording shooting attempts (successful and unsuccessful) and provide performers with more detailed feedback following the game.

This could also include other invasion game-related skills such as passing, tackling, turn-overs, and dribbling.

Advanced scoring analysis: There are a number of applications which would allow students to obtain more detailed data related to scoring.

This could include analysis of a cricket match where the non-participant records the direction of scoring runs, and the frequency of scoring.

CHAPTER SUMMARY

- Technology should be embedded into the culture of your teaching, not just form a 'bolt-on' to your practice.
- Ensure that the ICT being used is contributing to the learning experience, and avoid things that may cause a distraction or be detrimental to your students' progress.
- Allowing students to develop their ICT skills is part of the wider responsibilities of a teacher.
- Try to use technology platforms that students are already engaged with, such as social media, to improve communication.
- Use ICT to increase opportunities for students to collaborate, work independently, and critically analyse their work.

TALKING POINTS

1. How can you ensure that any use of ICT is purposeful, and not causing unnecessary distractions within your lesson?
2. What ICT skills can be developed within PE?
3. How could you use social media to positively impact learning and progress?
4. When would it be appropriate to use video analysis within a practical PE lesson?

9 Ensuring good behaviour in PE lessons

This chapter will discuss different strategies which can be used to create a positive learning environment for all students within Physical Education. With the potentially hazardous nature of some topics within the subject, the management of student behaviour is paramount.

Different methods of behaviour management will be discussed, and examples of how to develop professional relationships with students will be identified (including common behaviours which are seen within PE). This chapter will also make reference to some strategies that are relevant to students with behavioural/learning difficulties.

Strategies:

* Initial high expectations
* Clear, and agreed boundaries (routines)
* Progressive sanctions (behaviour policies)
* Encourage independent learning
* Positive body language
* Reducing 'teacher talk'
* Setting work that is adequate, and appropriately challenging.

Teaching within a practical environment brings with it numerous potential issues. This is one of the main reasons that Physical Education is unique. Controlling challenging students outside the parameters of the classroom can be difficult, with some issues leading to health and safety concerns. Many of the aspects of behaviour can be managed to maximise the learning experience of our classes. The first step towards achieving this is to have high initial expectations of students.

High expectations

One of the most important elements of any lesson is what we do within the first few seconds – setting the scene for the lesson and promoting curiosity about the knowledge about to be taught.

For me, this begins at the doors of the changing rooms, greeting each and every student as they enter my learning environment. The greeting sounds trivial, and possibly insignificant, but this signals the start of my lesson.

This conforms to the work of Ivan Pavlov in the early 1900s with regards to classical conditioning, where a stimulus is directly associated with a learnt response. In this case, your greeting will facilitate the change in attitude of the student and signal the start of your lesson. High expectations of behaviour and application will be expected as with any other lesson within the school.

Another common theme within Physical Education is the mystery surrounding the 'sick note'.

Students from over the years have used this process to avoid topics that are less enjoyable, which brings with it a number of potential issues. It is imperative that all students within your class are involved in the learning experience regardless of physical health.

Obviously, there are situations which will make this more difficult, such as the student walking with crutches due to a broken leg. One policy I have found to be very effective is ensuring that all students get changed into their PE kit, regardless of their health/fitness issues. This creates a change in attitude for the student that they will still be a part of the lesson.

There will be circumstances where this is not always appropriate, but where possible, it can send a powerful message to your students. A variety of roles and tasks can be conducted by the 'non-participant', such as officiating, coaching, organising and choreographing, which have all in recent years been a part of GCSE Physical Education assessments.

However, potential issues can arise with this strategy if the student is not engaged. Therefore, it is important to ensure the student can both access the work, and remain suitably challenged so as to not be a distraction for others within your class.

Example of application

During a basketball lesson, you have a student with a broken wrist, and therefore unable to participate in a performing capacity. The obvious tasks can easily be created for the student, such as scoring fixtures, or completing observation and analysis tasks. However, a lot of these tasks require a certain level of prior knowledge – would a low-ability Year 9 student be able to confidently and competently officiate a game?

For me, some of the best tasks are observation and analysis tasks associated with processes within the activity, rather than outcomes. Instead of a student being tasked with the scoring of games (a tedious/unchallenging task), the student can be tasked with basic analysis tasks linked to the lesson objectives – for example, number of completed passes, percentage of successful free-throws or success rates of dribbling.

Clear and agreed boundaries

Setting clear expectations to the classes you teach is so important. This sets the tone for your teaching, and provides no 'grey areas' which could be abused by misbehaviour.

Ensuring good behaviour in PE lessons

So, it is paramount to set these clear and precise expectations at the earliest possible point. For example, if you were to allow students to talk over each other during a class or group discussion unchallenged, then this behaviour is likely to be repeated.

By intervening early, students within the class will be aware that this is inappropriate, and the chances of this behaviour being repeated will be reduced.

Boundaries are important and need to be considered for Physical Education are as follows:

- Arriving to lessons on time, and in an appropriate manner
- Ensuring that all kit/equipment has been brought to the lesson
- Showing respect to others throughout all phases of the lesson (teachers and fellow students)
- Behaving in a responsible and safe manner
- Classwork is to be completed to the best of the students' ability
- All work is completed by the required, and agreed timeframe.

A formal routine is very important, to provide all students with the boundaries they are expected to behave within. Initially, it is important to establish these expectations yourself, but there are situations where you can utilise the students within the process to ensure they agree and 'buy-in' to the rules of your classroom.

One successful strategy with many groups is the creation of a class 'code' – this creates the illusion that the students are deciding the boundaries for behaviour, but can be an effective strategy to ensure students adhere to the agreement. Here's how it works . . .

Your first job is to highlight the 'non-negotiable' rules in which the students have no flexibility. This will include required kit/ equipment, such as studded footwear and gumshields. You may also wish at this point to underline protocols which support your high expectations – for example, what is the protocol for students when they forget an item of kit?

120

This will set the tone for your classroom 'code of conduct' while providing a platform for you to reinforce rules and avoid any confrontations which could be avoided via this process.

Following this, you can now move on to behaviours in which students can have an input, and with some well-guided questioning, students will hopefully come up with rules you would have done anyway. This could include: 'What do you think should happen if someone talks over somebody else?'

Pupils will be able to articulate basic behaviours and repercussions very easily without much of your input. Responses will hopefully lead to students identifying that talking over others (be it you as the teacher, or their peers) is unacceptable and will lead to agreed sanctions.

This strategy also creates the impression that the students are deciding, or at least involved in decisions which will create ownership and adherence to the boundaries.

However, great care needs to be taken with this approach, and it would not be suitable to groups that display moderate or frequent behaviour issues. This would also be the case for teaching younger year groups, particularly those that have recently joined your school.

Once these boundaries have been established, and agreed, your focus as the teacher can then turn to promoting learning within the lesson. However, you must assume that behaviour will still need to be managed by you constantly. For this to be effective, you will need to be vigilant throughout all stages of the lesson, and be in a position to ensure all learners maintain the high standards you have outlined. This will mean having a presence within your entire teaching space, a difficult task when faced with a wet and windy day on the sports field.

The most effective way to do this is learning to allow students time to complete tasks independently – this creates you time to survey the entire class, ensuring all students are on-task and work is being completed to the standards you expect.

Although we are currently discussing the management of behaviour, it is worth noting that this strategy also creates excellent opportunities to provide students with feedback. While you are travelling around your teaching space, vigilantly ensuring that students remain on-task, feedback can be given to students to enhance their work, reinforce teaching points/learning objectives, and giving praise to highlight progress and positive behaviours.

But what happens when students are off-task? How do you act to ensure all of the work set is completed within your lesson?

If you have been successful in spotting behaviour discrepancies, these can often be dealt with very easily via small preventative actions. For example, in some cases, a 'stare' at offenders can sometimes be enough to deter further off-task behaviour. Other actions could include reminding the students of the earlier agreed boundaries, questioning the students understanding of instructions to ensure that misunderstanding is not to blame, or a calm initial warning may be required.

Progressive sanctions

That brings us to the question: What happens if misbehaviour continues beyond the earlier intervention? In my view, behaviour policies can at times be over-complicated. If students do not know and understand sanctions, then misbehaviour will be more likely to occur.

Take our previous example:

You have presented your students with a task, and have used this opportunity to allow the students to work independently while you roam your teaching space to maintain and manage the lesson. A student that was misbehaving has been initially spoken to and encouraged to remain on task, yet as soon as you turn your back, the misbehaviour continues.

It is important to deal with this rapidly as failure to act may create more severe misbehaviours later in the lesson.

At this stage, the misbehaviour will need to be dealt with using a firmer response. However, it is important to not do this publicly – this more often than not will result in the student becoming embarrassed and could result in them being even more disengaged within your lesson.

I would suggest that at this point, a private conversation away from earshot of other students is probably needed. This will need to include that the behaviours being seen are inappropriate, and it may be powerful to highlight more severe sanctions if their misbehaviour was to continue.

However, the most important factor at this stage of the behaviour management is following-up with the more severe sanction if the misbehaviour persists. If this is the case, then the student will need to be given the more severe sanction, most typically in the form of detentions.

It is important that this is implemented by you as the teacher. In most cases, a conversation in the student's own time following the lesson is punishment enough, but longer detentions can be used if the behaviour continues to persist.

Other powerful sanctions for persistent misbehaviours includes a quick phone-call home to discuss the student's behaviour with parents/guardians.

It is also important to remember that there are other colleagues available to support you with misbehaviour, particularly at the start of your career – and using these people is not a sign of weakness. Sometimes, the support of a more senior member of staff to reinforce your message can be very powerful, and will be seen by the student in question as a more severe sanction. However, it is important that you remain involved within the process.

Simply passing on behaviour issues to another member of staff will not sufficiently deal with the issue, if anything, it will inform the student that you do not have control of the situation. This could be in the form of an apology from the student following the sanction from another member of staff, or you being present when they discuss the misbehaviour – either way, you as their teacher are responsible and in control of the issue.

Encourage independent learning

This strategy places responsibility for behaviour on to the students. They will need to learn to complete their work without direct input from you, manage their time, while ensuring they remain on-task in order to complete the work set.

As discussed previously, this style of teaching also presents opportunities for you to provide feedback, give additional support, or formally assess the work being completed.

The inclusion of this responsibility is commonly well-received by students, if the tasks being presented to them are fully understood and pitched at the correct level.

Therefore, checking understanding of your instructions prior to starting a task in this way will be very important. This can be done quickly with some closed-answered questions, or via use of a student demonstration.

But there are many tasks that students of most ages/abilities should be able to complete with ease, such as completing their own warm-ups at the start of a lesson, or applying basic skills to small-sided competitive situations.

Positive body language

Students are very astute – they are able to identify quickly when a teacher lacks confidence as often seen when classes are led by supply teachers, who may lack effective behaviour management skills.

I remember one of the first pieces of advice that was given to me regarding my presence when travelling around a new school: '*always make eye-contact with students, and walk the corridors with confidence and assertiveness*'.

A lot can be said for this, it is easy to put your head down, and hastily make your way through the school, but having a positive presence is powerful. I use this opportunity to speak to the students, remind them of extra-curricular opportunities, and always pick-up on low-level misbehaviours – conforming to my high expectations.

For example, if you are walking behind a group of students and one of them drops some litter, do you challenge the behaviour? Or ignore it and pick up the litter? The answer should be to challenge the behaviour – this doesn't need to be a 'telling-off' as such, but informs the student that the behaviour you have seen is not appropriate, reinforcing your expectations.

The same goes for within your lessons – having positive, confident body language is important. One key skill to develop quickly is the ability to use a whistle. Strong, assertive whistle blows when required are useful – particularly when an unsafe behaviour needs to be dealt with quickly to avoid injury.

Reducing 'teacher talk'

Throughout my career I have observed many lessons implemented by teachers new to the profession. One of the most common causes of misbehaviour in these lessons is boredom. It is an easy trap to fall into when relatively new to teaching to feel like you need to 'over-teach' or 'over-explain' instructions.

PE is a practical subject; no students will want to be standing around for long periods of time listening to one person speak. Therefore, developing strategies to reduce the amount of time you talk at the students will be useful.

Resources such as task cards can be effective to do this – while also presenting opportunities for the students to work independently.

An example of this could include instructions for a task, such as a basic skill-development drill. Lengthy continuous prose from the teacher will lead to disengagement, and students will easily lose key pieces of information, which may result in tasks not being accessible.

High-achieving students will be presented with an opportunity to lead activities which are pre-planned – therefore developing basic leadership skills (such as self-confidence, communication, etc.).

An alternative to this will be to present the information to small groups and allow them time to collaborate and work out the task, presenting you with an opportunity to deal with any misunderstandings, and provide support to individual students appropriately.

Pre-planning instructions which are short, sharp and precise will no doubt be advantageous. Visual aids and prompts can also help reduce the amount of direction you will need to give students prior to them completing the task.

Setting work that is adequate, and appropriately challenging

There is another common reason for misbehaviour within lessons. When work set is completed quickly by students, off-task behaviour will follow as the students will no longer be engaged in the task.

This is usually the case when the work set is pitched at a level that is too easy for the class – students will find this tedious which can lead to issues, which you will then need to manage.

The same can be said when work set is pitched too high for students to access. For example, if a group of students are asked to devise an activity to help improve a skill with very little subject-knowledge, they will soon become disengaged due to the lack of success they can get from the task without teacher intervention.

This will all be avoided with appropriate planning prior to teaching, and designing tasks that can be easily adapted to increase, or decrease difficulty.

It goes without saying that knowing your classes is very important. All students will have different needs, will learn in different ways and will be engaged through different types of tasks. Students with specific learning needs will need to be catered for appropriately to ensure they can complete tasks set within your lesson.

CHAPTER SUMMARY

- Behaviour needs to be managed, not avoided.
- Effective planning and preparation prior to teaching can reduce a number of common misbehaviours which can occur within practical environments.
- Rules and boundaries are non-negotiable – it is your classroom and you are in control.
- All misbehaviour needs to be dealt with quickly, and appropriately.
- Use sanctions which are progressively more severe in cases where bad behaviour continues.

TALKING POINTS

1. What are the common causes of 'bad behaviour' within lessons?
2. What rules/boundaries do you use? And how do you ensure these are enforced?
3. Consider a minor occurrence of misbehaviour (such as off-task chatting), how would you deal with this within a lesson?
4. How can you ensure that behaviour sanctions are fair and consistent?

10 Using action research to improve practice

Action research refers to investigations which are used to solve problems or create a platform for reflection. If used appropriately, it can be a very successful way to highlight strengths, areas for improvement, or to reinforce the impact that some of our work has on young people.

Research can be small-scale enquiries, or form part of a larger project – such as research which may form part of a Master's degree, or a segment of training.

More importantly though, these investigations can be used to improve what we do in the classroom, on the sports field and within our own roles. Conclusions highlighted within our research can improve individual teaching practice, teaching across your department, and highlight how PE can be used as a tool for 'whole-school improvement'.

In this chapter, I will discuss a range of research ideas which can be used easily, alongside the teaching role, to inform practice and increase reflection opportunities.

Each research concept will also include some examples of how it can be implemented for PE and school sport.

Participation audits

One key aspect of a successful PE and school sport programme within a school is its extra-curricular provision. But how do we maximise its impact?

It is common to see that a school's extra-curricular timetable is more often than not, saturated with a wide range of sporting activities and opportunities.

Analysis of extra-curricular participation data is an effective way of determining whether current provision is effective.

For example, how many students attend each club/activity? If 30 or more students attend a club at one time, is staffing sufficient, or can a wider workforce be utilised to improve the provision?

Participation data will also highlight any clubs/activities that are poorly attended. If this is the case, it would surely be a better use of a teacher's time to provide an alternative activity which may attract a higher number of students to engage with additional physical activity.

Trends in the participation data will also highlight which activities students are engaged with, and could even inform the activities that are taught within the PE curriculum.

Exploring the potential of including some 'alternative' activities, such as tchoukball or korfball, within curriculum time may increase participation in some alternative extra-curricular provisions.

Participation data alone can highlight trends and patterns, which can be used to determine basic conclusions. Deeper analysis will allow you to gain an insight into which students are participating in extra-curricular activities.

Example 1: Analysing registers at extra-curricular clubs to determine what students are attending.

It is not uncommon to see similar students attending a wide range of provisions. Just participation data would not show the range of students engaged with additional activities. If the same students attend most activities on offer, it may highlight

129

that alternative activities may be an effective way to attract a wider variety/higher number of students.

Example 2: Analysing the range of students attending extra-curricular clubs.

In relation to 'whole-school' attainment, data which displays the range of students accessing activities beyond the school day can be very powerful.

This data could include the number of students participating in extra-curricular sport from a range of backgrounds, including students from disadvantaged backgrounds, special educational needs, those who speak English as a second language, gender, etc.

Example 3: Analysing the impact of curriculum provision on extra-curricular participation.

If curriculum time is going to be used to promote extra-curricular activities, analysis of participation data following the intervention will demonstrate the impact these provisions are having.

For example: Is using a local sports coach an effective way of attracting more students to attend an activity? Or is the inclusion of 'alternative' activities within the taught PE programme an effective way of increasing interest in additional physical activity?

Learning walks

This refers to a professional development strategy, which involves informal observations of other teachers during their lessons.

Learning walks can be advantageous at any stage of a teaching career – but can be particularly useful at the beginning as you will gain an insight into different teaching methods, pedagogy and behaviour management strategies.

It is important to ensure that the observations remain informal. This will provide a realistic insight into another person's teaching. It is also effective to try learning walks outside of your subject specialism. For example, behaviour management strategies within a classroom can be very different to the sports field.

An effective learning walk may contain some of the following features:

1. **Paired learning walks**: Learning walks which are conducted in pairs. This will provide a platform for developmental conversations based on the observations being conducted.

    Teaching strategies can be collaboratively critiqued and analysed to give you more insights on the observations.

2. **Specific focus**: Ensure the learning walk has a particular focus.

    For example, it may be useful to observe behaviour management strategies, differentiation techniques, use of questioning, or the impact of assessment.

    It may be that subject knowledge is the focus, and observing a variety of different teachers delivering similar topics may provide a useful comparison of teaching methods.

3. **A variety of staff**: It is important that you visit a wide range of staff during your learning walks.

    Without this feature, observations and more importantly your insights will be restricted. This does need to be balanced to ensure you spend sufficient amounts of time with each teacher, and will depend on the lesson duration used in the school.

4. **Speak to students**: Throughout your observations, try speaking to individual students about the lesson.

    This provides an extra insight into how effective students interpret different strategies. Although, care will need to be taken to ensure you do not have a negative effect on the students focus in the lesson.

    Questioning students on what they are learning, and assessing their levels of engagement can be very useful.

5. **Feedback**: Find an efficient method of feeding back to your colleagues following your learning walk.

    This is not to be confused with direct feedback to the staff you observed, but a holistic overview to highlight any of your findings.

It is important to remember that this is an informal, developmental approach, and teachers need to feel comfortable, and confident that this is not an assessment of their teaching.

Exploring the possibility of using a small segment of a department meeting could be an effective way to do this.

6. **Next steps**: Following completion of your learning walk, try to formalise some next steps.

What can you use from your observations within your own practice? Where there any strategies or ideas used that you could trial in your own teaching?

Questioning audits

As with the participation audit, this investigative research involves the collection of data – but this time all centred around Assessment for Learning.

Using 'Bloom's Taxonomy of Questioning', or another similar hierarchy of questioning system, allows us to categorise questioning which can be used to reflect on teaching strategies.

A simple 'tally chart' system can be employed easily to obtain raw data regarding the questioning used by a teacher within lessons. This would allow you to reflect on the frequency of the different levels of questioning used.

Practical example: When teaching an activity with moderate to high safety implications, such as javelin, it is often seen that our teaching styles become very autocratic and teacher-led.

Although this teaching style has been adopted to reduce safety concerns, our questioning will need to be altered to ensure the learning experience for students is not reduced.

This strategy will also ensure that lower-order questions, such as knowledge recall or closed questions, are not over used within lessons – and we stretch our students via the use of more challenging questioning.

It can also be an insightful process for other teachers to receive informal feedback regarding the frequency of their questioning throughout activities.

For the more inexperienced teacher, it is a useful investigation which focusses solely on this form of formative assessment. Allowing you to gain knowledge about different questioning strategies, and how best to challenge students with questioning within a practical environment.

Focus groups

One of the most powerful research tools at a teacher's disposal is our students.

Focus groups are a method of data collection like interviews, but allow students to respond to questions, or discussions in small groups – and provide a wealth of information.

Using students for insight, teaching reflection, and to improve current provisions can be very beneficial. This could also be achieved via questionnaires, but allowing students to verbally discuss topics and opinions can provide a lot more information.

Example 1: Increasing female participation in extra-curricular clubs.

Using focus groups to investigate strategies which can positively influence female students' engagement in extra-curricular activities will allow you to gain an insight into the barriers which may be preventing them participating.

Female participation in school sport is a common concern in a number of secondary schools. Focus groups will provide a platform for discussion where female students can discuss potential provisions which may have a positive effect.

Example 2: Decreasing the effects of transition within Physical Education.

PE tends to produce certain 'myths' with regards to the transition to secondary school. Using focus groups in this context will allow you to gain an insight into what concerns younger students about PE and school sport prior to transfer, and hopefully enable you to dispel any myths and reduce the potentially negative effects of transition.

Allowing students to discuss any causes of concern to them, such as changing room arrangements, kit expectations, strict teaching methods or new activities will allow you to reassure others, and create alternative provisions which may improve students' confidence in PE.

Example 3: Creating a student council group for school sport.

This provision would allow you to create a steering group of students which could be used to inform future provisions of your department.

Using students to discuss what extra-curricular activities are most effective, what students feel comfortable wearing within lessons, additional opportunities that would gain increased engagement are all topics which will rely heavily on student insights.

The most effective part of this process, is the fact that the students involved feel empowered and part of the development of the department – a powerful message which will have a positive effect on the engagement of other students.

Case studies

This method of action research is mainly focused on your findings from any investigation – but as important as the research itself.

Case studies provide a method of disseminating your findings, and highlight the impact of your/other's work. This is also important in reference to 'whole-school impact' – where your investigations from PE and school sport can be used to influence the staff, teaching and provisions across the whole school.

Example 1: Student case studies.

Consider a provision you have put in place to improve attainment of a highly-able sports student, potentially a student who is actively competing at an international level. What provisions can you put in place to support this student?

Responses to this question could include extended deadlines on coursework, flexible timetables or an adapted PE provision within curriculum time.

Whatever your chosen response is, using a case study template to describe the impact of this support can be very useful. This will present others with ideas of how to support similar students, and create a 'best practice' model.

Example 2: Impact of daily physical activity.

One of the key battles which PE and school sport currently face is justifying the subjects time on the school's curriculum.

Highlighting the position of PE, and the impact the subject has is continually becoming more important. As PE practitioners, we all know the benefits of physical activity for our students, but can we use case studies to emphasise this?

Creating a case study which investigates the impact of daily physical activity on student attainment would provide effective evidence to support the importance of PE.

Recent examples of this include projects like 'The Daily Mile', which involves students completing a mile run every day, and measuring the impact this has in the classroom.

Using 'action research' to improve your teaching

The important thing with all action research is deciding how the data and findings of your research can be used.

It is important to devise ways in which you can use your findings within your own practice. This could be as simple as trialling some different behaviour management techniques, or alternative questioning techniques.

Try to find effective ways of disseminating your findings to others, this could be within your department, or to other teachers.

CHAPTER SUMMARY

- Action research is a method of investigating present issues within education, to which solutions can be trialled or reflections can be made regarding current provisions.
- Action research can take many forms, and should be used alongside your role.
- Research can be used to inform your practice, increase reflection or share ideas with others.
- Ensure that if observing others that the process remains informal, it is important to observe practice within realistic environments for it to be useful.
- Provide feedback to others on your findings – you may be able to inform the practice of others, and this can form a good platform for developmental discussions.
- Use your action research findings to produce 'next steps', and decide how your findings can enhance your practice.

TALKING POINTS

1. What small-scale research could you use within your teaching to improve your practice?
2. How can you effectively inform others within your school about any of your findings?
3. What considerations would you make when interviewing students within a focus group?
4. If you are collecting data, how do you plan to analyse your findings?

11 PE as a tool for improving transition/transfer

When investigating attainment and progress of students within PE, a common trend which was highlighted within the HMI report (2008) suggests that some students' learning plateaus, or at times dips following the transfer to a new school.

So, what do we mean by the terms 'transition' and 'transfer'? Transition (pupils progressing from one year to the next) and transfer (students moving from one school to another) is an integral part of our students learning experience – and is an important factor within our schools.

Most schools prior to transfer will send data deemed relevant to create a benchmark upon the students' arrival at your school. This data may include:

- SAT scores
- Reading levels
- Attainment levels (assessed by previous teacher)
- Special educational needs (may be in the form of an individual education plan)
- Able, Gifted and Talented information.

Even with the data listed above, are we really in a position to effectively teach Physical Education? The answer is generally no,

PE as a tool for improving transition/transfer

and time is then needed to be spent on re-teaching skills to ensure all students are provided with the tools to access our subject.

What data would be more useful for Physical Education? Here are a few ideas which can increase your knowledge of students prior to them joining your school:

- Has the student been involved in any sports leadership?
- What school sports clubs do they regularly attend?
- What community sports clubs do they attend?
- Do the students enjoy PE?
- Do the students display high confidence levels within PE lessons?
- Basic physical attributes (basic fitness test data, athletics results, etc.)
- A short teacher comment (much more useful than a subjective level description).

Although the collection of this data may seem overwhelming to teachers of the previous school, it may be that a meeting prior to the transfer will allow most of this information to be given to you, rather than emailing spreadsheets which can be seen as tedious and time consuming.

However, this is not the only reason which can be associated with the plateau/dip in student attainment following transfer.

Physical Education is a subject which can create anxiety for students prior to joining a new school, particularly the movement to secondary school. A number of strategies can be used within PE to reduce these effects and some ideas will be outlined for the following:

- Passports/portfolios
- Producing a video
- Regular visits for transferees
- Engage young people in conversations about transfer/transition

- Displays
- Visiting feeder schools prior to transfer
- Talent-spotting activities.

Passports/portfolios

These can be presented in many formats, but will need to involve two key principles: what information highlights the students' knowledge/skills, and ownership from the student.

This will also depend on how the previous school assesses units-of-work. If activities are graded using levels, this is information which can be provided easily to highlight strengths and areas for improvement for each student. An important consideration using this method, however, will be highlighting the activity area that the information is associated with.

High-level rugby performers tend to have an excellent skill set, for example footwork, agility, spatial awareness, co-ordination and power to name a few. More importantly, the sport-specific skills they have developed can be difficult to transfer to other activities (e.g. a drop kick in rugby compared to a volley in football). Therefore, if the student is assessed using football as the activity area, the information provided can be very easily misinterpreted.

The key element of this process is student involvement. The students will need to individually determine evidence they wish to be added and do a lot of this independently. This could include information such as extra-curricular clubs attended, recent sporting achievements, and leadership opportunities.

This process is not only useful in the transfer process, but can also provide good evidence of student progress, if used in a way that provides students to self-assess the knowledge and skills they have developed. It can provide insight into self-assessments, and an understanding of how their bodies react to physical activity, or possibly key technical points of skills being taught.

Producing a video

Providing students with a 'virtual tour' of the environment they are about to move to can be very powerful. The facilities that most secondary schools have for Physical Education tend to eclipse those that the pupils would be used to – which provides a great opportunity to get students excited about what to expect at their new school.

Inspirational clips that show exciting PE lessons, engaged students and positive attitudes can be added. An important factor to try and include within this is activities that the students may have not tried before, such as trampolining. This again will provide information about exciting opportunities within your department.

Protocols such as changing room procedures and where to find extra-curricular information can be addressed so that students know what to expect. The great thing about this process is that it provides an opportunity to dispel any 'myths' that may be present.

For example, a common concern for primary students prior to transfer is often protocols surrounding changing rooms and showers. These questions can be answered in the video, and better still can be answered by students that have recently been through the process who may have had similar concerns.

Insights from students that have more recently been through the transfer process can be a useful tool to reduce anxieties and answer queries. These pupils tend to relate easily to the pupils about to transfer. They can remember concerns or questions they had prior to moving schools, which more often than not, tend to be very similar.

Using young leaders from the primary school to produce the video can also provide an opportunity to develop confidence prior to transfer. Key messages can then be provided by the transfer school, and distributed to the primary students by their peers.

Other important pieces of information which you may wish to consider within the video include PE kit, equipment needed and possibly an introduction to the PE staff who will be teaching them.

Regular visits for transferees

Any opportunities than can be created for students to visit their future school will be advantageous. Engaging them in exciting activities which will leave them feeling like they cannot wait to join your school.

Most schools will arrange at least one opportunity for pupils to visit their new schools prior to transfer, but time constraints usually do not allow much time for PE departments to dispel any of the untruths previously mentioned.

More regular visits will obviously be more advantageous. Exploring the possibility of secondary school staff teaching a unit-of-work prior to transfer would have many positive outcomes, such as getting to know the students first-hand.

The students transferring will get many more advantages from an experience like this. Changing protocols can actually be experienced, as well as meeting the members of staff who will teach them in the next academic year.

Secondary schools that have a number of feeder schools may find opportunities like this more difficult. However, there are still a number of provisions you can put into place.

Hosting events such as inter-school competitions will have the same desired effects. PE department staff can be present, young leaders from the school can be used to support the event and the environment they are moving to will be experienced.

One of the less obvious advantages of this method is the strengthening of the professional relationships between the staff at both the feeder and secondary school. Both schools will be aware of the importance of this liaison and this process can also allow opportunities to standardise assessments between the two schools and improve consistency of data.

Engage young people in conversations about transfer/transition

Some schools make use of interviews, which can include parents/ guardians to discuss and answer any questions or concerns the students may have. However, a more effective way to do this is using students.

As previously discussed, the involvement of students within the transfer process is paramount. The nervousness of moving schools can be effectively reduced via dialogue between students moving to the new school and the students that have recently gone through the same process.

In the first instance, it is important to discover the questions that the transferring students may have: Do they know what activities will be taught? What kit do they need? Where do they go for their PE lessons?

The use of small focus groups led by either a teacher at the secondary school, or better still, a student that has experienced the transfer themselves, can create an environment for students to securely discuss their concerns. Grouping students together can promote confidence in itself, and hopefully will provide a platform for them to discuss factors that may create anxiety.

Allaying rumours which circulate about PE is very important, so it is critical to reinforce that all questions/queries the students may have are useful and important. But can more be done with this information?

Displays

A very simple, but effective, method of disseminating the information drawn from the discussions described above is via display boards.

The questions put forward by the students about to transfer can be outlined and answered in a clear, concise format. Information

142

such as kit, timetables, curriculums and expectations can all be included for students to digest independently.

This could also very easily be produced and displayed in the primary school prior to the transfer to put the pupils' minds at rest over any initial worries.

As with the regular visits, there is also an opportunity with this method to 'showcase' the exciting things students will expect at their new school. Extra-curricular opportunities, trips and visits, recent successes and examples of engaging lessons can all be included to create excitement and anticipation, rather than the often-found nervousness.

Another key consideration of this method is engaging students with the display. So what makes a good display? Here are some considerations when creating your display boards:

- Use of key words
- Short and precise messages
- Eye-catching images
- Bright and bold colours
- Position in a prominent area.

It is also worth considering using students who have recently left the feeder school.

For example, photos of these students engaged and happy within their new environment can be very settling, and the students from the primary school should remember the faces on the display and will be able to relate to the images more effectively.

Visiting feeder schools prior to transfer

Is it possible for a member of staff at the receiving school to be released to visit feeder schools prior to the transfer of students?

This could take many forms, for example joining a residential trip, accompanying a team to a local fixture/event or supporting PE lessons alongside the primary school teacher.

143

In order for this to occur, it may be that school calendars need to be shared between the schools in advance. This should allow you to arrange appropriate opportunities well in advance.

It is often easier in secondary schools for appropriate times to be created for these exchanges to occur. Activity weeks, work experience or when students leave following examinations may present opportunities for secondary staff to visit feeder schools.

There are many advantages of this method. Firstly, the secondary school staff will get to know transferring students personally, an important factor already discussed. Furthermore, the students about to transfer will get to know the teachers of their new school – a variable that can at times cause nervousness for the pupils.

However, this method can also have a significant effect on teaching. Team teaching with our colleagues from the feeder schools can help our own subject knowledge, particularly having more insights into the experiences the students have had previous to them being taught by you.

Furthermore, your expertise within Physical Education as a 'subject-specialist' can be very useful for the primary school staff. Transferring subject knowledge or different activities/methods of teaching will be a developmental experience all-round.

Collaborative assessments can also be done between the staff of the two schools, therefore reducing the inconsistencies in the grading of students.

Talent-spotting activities

Knowledge of the most-able students you are about to receive is very useful. At times, these students will require bespoke support that PE specialists can provide effectively.

Talent identification is prominent in sport, and many of the characteristics can be transferred into Physical Education. For example, exploring the possibility of these students visiting the secondary school for a 'talent-camp' like experience will be to the benefit of the students themselves, as well as increasing knowledge of each student for the transfer school.

A six-week programme addressing areas associated with top-level sport (e.g. time management, diet and strength and conditioning) will provide this group of students with generic skills which can help them within their individual disciplines.

If this is organised and run by you as the secondary school teacher, this will present you with regular contact to get to know each student.

Other successful models have made use of multi-skill events to collect data to identify 'Gifted and Talented' students prior to transfer. Basic activities that measure key components of fitness (e.g. agility, speed and reaction time) can give a profile of the students' current performance levels, and can be used when preparing to teach these students.

However, it is important to ensure that the transferring students do not see this as 'testing'. This could have severe negative consequences and lead to a decrease in confidence levels. Fitness tests should be avoided, and more creative activities employed to ensure that the pupils involved are not only benefiting from the experience, but also enjoying it.

CHAPTER SUMMARY

- Consider what data you need in order to plan effective lessons prior to transfer.
- What can you do to ensure that students are not being taught content that has been previously been covered?
- Investigate what factors students may be effected by prior to transfer, and dispel any myths or rumours.
- Create opportunities to increase your knowledge of the students you will be teaching following transfer.

TALKING POINTS

1. How do you think students feel when transferring to secondary school?
2. How might these feelings affect PE?
3. What previous data would be useful to you prior to your planning?
4. What creative ways can you easily develop to improve the transfer process for your students?

12 Leadership for learning

In this chapter, we will explore what leadership means. We will look at how it can enhance the quality of your lessons and also the opportunities for students beyond the classroom. Finally, we will look at some practical ways to harness student leadership more directly.

Developing student leadership is important to us as PE teachers. It can bring many advantages to our students – within and around the lessons we teach.

But what is 'leadership'?

The term is used within a variety of contexts, whether it is in education, or within other careers.

Leadership in its most basic form refers to the actions of someone to influence others towards a common goal – and if used appropriately, can be a very powerful tool to the PE teacher.

Consider teaching an activity, and one of your students within your class is performing the sport at an elite level. Can you realistically stretch this student within their sport?

That depends. What you can do is challenge the student in different ways, and using leadership is a great example.

Our elite performer could be used as a coach, leading activities for the class, or providing peers with technical feedback drawing upon their knowledge within the activity.

Could the student work with some of the more, or less-able students within the activity? This will hopefully accelerate the rate of progress these students are making within your lesson.

Is there any technical, or tactical insights you could learn from the student? This should not be seen as a weakness, we are all forever expanding our subject knowledge, and some students would have years of experience in specialist activities – but we need to utilise this to improve our teaching.

Before using any of the strategies above, it is important that students are taught the basic skills and qualities to be an effective leader, but how can this be done effectively?

The following factors will need to be taught and developed in order for students to extend their leadership skills:

- Skills/qualities of a leader
- Leadership styles
- Roles and responsibilities.

Teaching the skills/qualities of a leader

There is no definitive list of the skills and qualities a leader should possess. However, there are many common characteristics that successful leaders display, which students should be able to identify.

Ask your students to consider a successful leader. This does not even need to be relevant to sport, but for example, let's say a student selects a successful football manager – such as Sir Alex Ferguson.

When reviewing the characteristics of this leader, students will be able to describe qualities they see as factors that contribute to them being a successful leader. These could include:

- *Communication*: Being able to communicate with their players while they are playing.
- *Confidence*: They make decisions, are not easily influenced by others and have confidence in their knowledge/ability.

- *Positive role model*: They display characteristics which makes players want to work for their leader.

- *Authoritative*: Players will need to respect them, follow their directions and respond to their instructions.

- *Empathy*: They will need to understand how others feel when they make decisions, and act on this appropriately.

There are many ways you can encourage students to identify appropriate skills/qualities:

- *Drawing/annotating the perfect leader*: Allowing your students to be creative and draw a 'perfect' leader.

  Responses could include a person with 'eyes in the back of their head' to demonstrate observation skills, or big ears to indicate being a good listener.

- *Review a leader within a lesson*: Ask a student to complete a basic leadership task, such as leading a warm up or simple skill development exercise.

  Following the activity, question the students on the leader's qualities: Did they communicate effectively? Were their instructions clear? Were you all motivated by the leader, and how did they do this?

- *Create acronyms*: These can be excellent wall displays, and very powerful to refer to when developing student leadership. Students will be able to independently, or within groups, identify skills/qualities/statements which refer to success in leadership:

L –	Lead by example
E –	Encourage others
A –	Attention
D –	Determination to succeed
E –	Evaluate your leadership
R –	Respond to changing situations

S –   Speak loud and clearly

H –   Have faith in your ability

I –   Inspire others

P –   Perseverance.

Leadership styles

When teaching leadership styles, it may be helpful to refer to three main classifications: autocratic, democratic and laissez-faire.

- *Autocratic*: Here, the leader dictates to the group who does what, and when they do it.

  This style is a good starting point, for example, asking a student to lead a warm up to a small group. Other group members will follow the instructions of the selected leader, making very few decisions themselves.

- *Democratic*: The leader encourages others within the group to participate in the decision-making process, and the leader makes the final decision. This style works well within problem-solving tasks, such as orienteering activities.

  It can be very easily applied to invasion game lessons, where students are working within teams and need to apply tactics, or formations within game situations.

- *Laissez-faire*: This refers to letting the group get on with tasks in their own way. Leaders in this style tend to support group members when difficulties occur, but do not offer any direction or make any decisions.

  This style can only be used with students that have had prior leadership experience. Group goals are more difficult to achieve using this style as they are being supported with very little direction.

  This can be an effective way of avoiding your more-able students doing all of the decision making for others, and using your more-able leaders to support other students with decision-making processes.

But what is the most effective method of teaching these styles to your students?

Students will need to understand the expectations of a leader within each style, and which style is most appropriate for the context they will be leading.

Consider creating leadership tasks for students to complete, and allow them to decide which leadership style to apply in order to complete the task effectively:

- *Autocratic*: Leading a basic football session for Key Stage 1 students from a primary school.

  The leader will need to make decisions for the participants as they will probably lack appropriate skills/knowledge within the activity.

- *Democratic*: Leading our school's basketball team during a game, making decisions on positions, starting line-up and tactics for the game.

  The leader can ask team members for advice or their opinions, and can use all of this information to make a decision for the team to employ.

- *Laissez-faire*: Creating a gymnastics or dance routine within small groups to display learnt skills at the end of a unit of work.

  The leader will need to support others within the group to make decisions. All students within the group will need to contribute ideas to complete the task.

Sport Education (model of leadership)

This method of developing leadership allows students to work in collaboration in order to complete a given task. Students will be given roles, which need to be understood to ensure the group work effectively towards a common goal.

Leadership for learning

There are six roles, and students will need to have an understanding of each in order for the approach to work:

1. **Team captain**: This is the overall leader of the group, they make decisions towards completing the task, and oversee the other group members.

2. **Record keeper**: Collates data during the task. This could be results of tests, tallying attempts and converting to success rates, or keeping scores. This role also includes updating the team members on their progress.

3. **Equipment manager**: Oversees all of the equipment required by the group. This role will include collecting and returning equipment during the task/lesson. May also include pitch markings or overseeing the space the group is using.

4. **Referee**: Ensures that the rules/instructions/boundaries of the task are adhered to. It is important this person has a good understanding of the expectations of the task.

5. **Observer/evaluator**: Observes the progress of the group and reports back to the team captain. This role should include evaluating the groups progress, and suggesting ways the task can be completed more effectively.

6. **Player**: No additional assigned responsibilities – but a participating member of team. They must complete tasks given and collaborate with other group members.

Once these roles are understood by the students, this model can be a very effective way of encouraging your classes to work more independently.

The roles given can be very easily adapted and modified. You will need to consider what is needed for the students to complete the task being given. It is important to consider the ability of the group to ensure they will be able to participate in their given role.

Teamwork and collaboration are at the core of these activities – thus creating an environment to develop student leadership.

Students will need to rotate roles to vary their experiences, and further develop their leadership skills. It is worth you noting the roles each student inherits to ensure they get a broad experience in future tasks.

Not only is this an effective way of teaching with PE, but can be applied to any subject within your school.

Consider an English lesson where students are preparing a presentation. All of the roles can be allocated to group members, and the task can be completed in a similar manner to that of a practical PE lesson.

This model allows you to facilitate learning, rather than instructing and delivering. This creates more opportunities to provide your students with feedback, and assess their learning.

Before using this model, make sure that clear guidance and instructions are given to the students to enable them to work towards completing their given task. Rules and routines will need to be understood to ensure mistakes do not occur without your direct supervision.

Qualifications in leadership

Leadership is not currently a part of schools' formal qualification structures, but are ever present within schools as additional qualifications.

These qualifications are excellent ways of developing student leadership, while providing some extrinsic motivation to increase engagement.

Sports Leadership Award

Sports Leaders UK (operating name of the British Sports Trust) is a leading provider for leadership qualifications. They provide qualifications within Sport, but also within Dance, English and Mathematics.

The most effective way to start is with the Sports Leadership Award (Level 1 and 2). These qualifications can easily be implemented into your PE curriculum teaching, within their existing PE lessons.

Each course consists of a number of units, which will need to be delivered, alongside students logging their leadership hours to achieve the award.

Units within the awards will include:

- Developing leadership skills
- Planning, leading and evaluating sport/physical activity sessions
- Assist in planning and leading a sports/physical activity event.

The awards are updated regularly, but the fundamentals of the course will remain the same. Both levels will allow you to develop your students' leadership towards them applying their skills within their class, school or local community.

Assessments within the awards rely on students gathering evidence throughout their course. This can be work observed by you as their teacher, written work, or video/audio evidence.

Both courses require the students to be a minimum of 13 years old, and you will need to be accredited as a centre in order to deliver the qualification. Teacher/instructor courses are readily available to equip you with all of the knowledge you need to deliver the qualification in your school.

Duke of Edinburgh Award

This is another common course delivered in some secondary schools, which can be an effective way to engage students in leadership – particularly within their local community.

The award consists of three levels: Bronze, Silver and Gold. The main differences between each level is the minimum length of time they take to complete, how challenging they are, and the minimum age your students need to be to start the course.

One of the advantages of this course is that it is very bespoke to each student, and allows them to create their own targets and accomplishments. The award is split into four sections (five for the Gold award) which students will need to complete:

1. **Volunteering**: Students will need to actively seek and participate in volunteering. This can be selected by the student, and can be anything from working with a local residential home, to supporting a coach at a local sports club.

2. **Physical**: Each student will need to set themselves physical fitness challenges and have evidence of working towards their goals. This could be attending a fitness class each week, developing their skills in a team sport and increasing their physical capacity while rock climbing.

3. **Skills**: This section refers to each student developing their skills within a certain field. It could be something they already do, or something completely new. The focus of this is developing practical and social skills which contribute to the students' personal interests. Examples could include learning a musical instrument, or how to cook.

4. **Expedition**: Each student will need to plan and complete a practice and final expedition as part of a small team. Orienteering and hiking activities are common choices, and aim to develop communication and leadership skills.

5. **Residential** (Gold Award only): If students are working towards a Gold award, they will also need to complete a residential expedition. This is more challenging than the expedition experienced in the previous two levels.

Every student will need to log their progress and obtain evidence for each section of the course. This should be independently managed by the students, and overseen by the course leader.

National Governing Body (NGB) Awards

The organisations that lead individual sports also have coaching awards that will develop students' knowledge within that activity.

Level 1 coaching awards will cover basic coaching and leadership methods within the sport, and will increase students' knowledge of sport-specific skills and activities.

These awards can be very expensive and time consuming, and are not specifically designed for secondary school students. But they are effective ways of extending leadership skills of our most-able students.

NGBs also offer sport-specific courses which can support student leadership. These aim to help students' apply their leadership skills into a sporting context, with the aim of training people to lead others within the sport.

All of these qualifications are designed to further develop students' confidence and skills in leadership, but also act as effective ways to add to the pupils' CV, and look great when applying for employment or further education.

Whole-school leadership

A common trend of students that engage with leadership within PE, is to transfer these skills into other roles within the school.

School leadership models, such as prefect systems, will also allow students to apply their skills, and increase their confidence.

It is part of your role as their PE teacher to 'sign-post' students in the direction of these opportunities, and develop the necessary skills for them to fulfil these roles effectively.

As a subject, PE tends to create lots of opportunities for students to work with younger students, whether that is in your school, or in the community.

It is important to create these opportunities to ensure the students are being adequately challenged, and continue to further develop within this area of our subject.

There are numerous, and alternative ways this can be achieved:

- *Sports events*: Allowing students to plan, lead and deliver events within the school, such as supporting sports days and intra-school competitions.

- *Fixtures*: Providing opportunities for students to support some of your extra-curricular provisions, such as refereeing/umpiring lower school fixtures, doing the scoring table during basketball fixtures and coaching a younger year group team.

- *Primary school sport*: Supporting the PE/sport delivery in local primary schools.

- *Additional leadership roles*: Engaging students in a variety of roles, such as photographers, social media teams, scorers, data collectors, team coaches, kit organisers, etc.

International leadership

Most schools have a link with another school within a foreign country. It is common for students to travel to this partner as part of a school exchange – but can PE play a leading role within this provision?

Consider being presented with a sports leadership task that needs to be completed with a group of students who cannot speak your language. This would raise a challenge to most people, and is a very effective way to stretch our most-able leaders.

Some activities may also be less known by the exchange school students, such as Chinese students understanding cricket. This creates a difficult challenge to students which will advance their skills.

As a starting-point, sporting/physical activities that incorporate what we call 'global languages' will allow the students to develop relationships quickly, and build their confidence.

Good examples of these types of activity include dance activities which allow the students to collaborate, multi-sport/fitness activities or sports that are commonly known/taught in both schools.

Body language will be a particularly useful skill for the students to use when trying to communicate basic instructions. Demonstrations will also be vital for the participants to fully understand the task being presented – but these are skills our students will need to develop.

The hardest part of this process as the teacher, is to take a step-back. Be confident in allowing students to struggle and make mistakes, remember this is part of their learning process and they will need to reflect following the task.

CHAPTER SUMMARY

- Developing student leadership is at the core of PE.
- Consider teaching the qualities, skills and styles of leadership prior to students completing tasks.
- Leadership tasks are an effective way of challenging our most-able students, and using this to support our less-able students.
- Investigate additional courses/qualifications that could engage more students within your subject, and raise the profile of PE within your school.
- Leadership skills taught within PE can be easily transferred to whole-school projects/roles – be sure to make this explicit to students, and direct them towards additional opportunities.

TALKING POINTS

1. Consider a successful leader, what skills and qualities do they possess?
2. What ways can the leadership skills developed within PE be used within other subjects?
3. How can you develop leadership skills within a typical PE lesson?
4. What ways can you stretch your most-able leaders, within and outside of lessons?

13 Improving subject knowledge

One of the most common struggles for trainee teachers as they begin to teach Physical Education, is a lack of subject knowledge within certain activity areas.

A high number of trainee PE teachers come from sports coaching backgrounds, or have had experience within some form of sports coaching. For example, access to coaching football at grass-roots level is readily available within England.

Although generic coaching skills in sport can be transferred to other activities, there is still a need to 'know your stuff'. Would being a football coach allow you to adequately teach gymnastics within a secondary school?

But how much do you need to know to be sure you can teach effectively?

As a PE teacher, you are not expected to be an expert in all of the activities you are due to teach. However, you are expected to have sufficient knowledge for your lessons to be safe, purposeful and stretch/challenge all of the abilities present within your classes.

There are a number of ways you can improve your subject knowledge within PE, some of which you can do before your initial teacher training, and others you can do while within the occupation.

This chapter aims to give you some ideas that may help you within activity areas, which may need some additional support to improve your teaching practice.

Self-analysis of your needs

The first step to improving your PE-specific knowledge is to acknowledge what areas of the subject you need to address.

Do you have any sports coaching qualifications in activities? Or have you had any experience working with young people within sport?

Although these experiences may not be in a teaching environment, the knowledge you develop can still be easily used.

You will need to look at the subject content broadly – considering all of the activities which you may be required to teach.

The easiest way to do this, is to 'RAG' rate activities areas. This process requires you to self-assess your knowledge by using a colour-coding system:

- **Green (G)**: You are confident you have the knowledge to teach this activity across all ages you will be teaching.

- **Amber (A)**: You have some levels of knowledge, or previous experiences within this activity, but need additional support in order to teach adequately across different age groups.

- **Red (R)**: You have very little, or no knowledge within this activity area.

It is also worth considering the depth in knowledge you have within these activity areas. You may have had experience coaching a youth netball team, but would that allow you to have enough knowledge to teach a GCSE netball lesson?

Try to assess your knowledge by rating to the different age ranges you will be likely to teach:

- Key Stage 3 (KS3): Age 11–14

- Key Stage 4 (KS4): Age 14–16

- GCSE PE (KS4): Age 14–16, extended knowledge, generally high sporting ability.

Improving subject knowledge

You will then need to complete this audit across all of the activities you may have to deliver within the first stages of your teaching career. You may not know what activities this will include at this stage, so consider the main activities within a typical secondary PE programme:

Table 13.1 Example of a self-assessment proforma to highlight subject knowledge needs within some invasion games

Invasion games	KS3	KS4	GCSE
Football	G	G	A
Netball	A	R	R
Rugby	G	A	R
Hockey	G	G	A
Basketball	G	G	A
Volleyball	G	G	A

What does the information in Table 13.1 tell you?

For the vast majority of the listed activities, the individual has highlighted that they feel confident in teaching most of the activities at Key Stage 3 and 4.

Netball and Rugby are the exceptions to this, which highlights their first initial need.

Knowledge within the GCSE column is consistently rated 'amber' or 'red', which may require some research into specific GCSE criteria for these activities, or a deeper technical/tactical understanding of these activities to stretch students at this stage of their education.

When completing an analysis like this, it is important to ensure you are honest. This should be a useful, reflective process – not a sign of weakness, and if done correctly, it will be a useful tool to prepare you for your teacher training.

Invasion games tend to be the most popular activities in relation to trainee teachers' prior knowledge. Make sure you assess your knowledge in other activity areas, such as the ones in Table 13.2:

Table 13.2 Example of a self-assessment proforma to highlight subject knowledge needs within different activity areas

	KS3	KS4	GCSE
Striking and fielding			
Cricket	____	____	____
Rounders	____	____	____
Softball	____	____	____
Net/wall games			
Badminton	____	____	____
Tennis	____	____	____
Squash	____	____	____
Table tennis	____	____	____
Individual sports			
Athletics	____	____	____
Gymnastics	____	____	____
Dance	____	____	____
Trampolining	____	____	____
Alternative activities			
Handball	____	____	____
Orienteering	____	____	____
Fitness	____	____	____

Some activity areas may require you to analyse in further detail, such as athletics. Try splitting the activities up before you do your self-assessment, for example sprints, middle-distance running, long-distance running, jumps and throws.

Resources

The internet contains a wealth of information which can be used to help improve your subject knowledge, or give you some ideas when planning lessons.

It is well worth spending time prior to teaching a unit of work to familiarise yourself with sport-specific knowledge, drills, rules and terminology to aid your planning.

National Governing Body websites for each individual sport are a useful resource for researching official rules and regulations, local training opportunities and often include some resources (such as downloadable coaching ideas) which will be a good starting point when beginning your planning.

Examination boards also have their own unique web-based resources, which can be used to support teaching examination subjects within PE. These will include specifications (course content) and practice examination materials (past papers and answers).

Video-streaming sites (such as YouTube) can also be powerful tools. There are a number of ways these can be used to help aid your subject knowledge:

- *Ideas for activities within lessons*: These could be in the form of drills/activities which have been recorded as part of coaching sessions, or could be some progressive ideas to make activities more challenging.

- *Analysis of skills within sports*: Critical analysis of sports-specific skills are important to help you understanding common faults and possible corrections of techniques, which can improve a students' performance of a skill.

  These can also be useful for students themselves, to provide information to help them assess the performance(s) of other students (reciprocal learning).

- *Demonstrations*: There may be some activities or skills you cannot effectively demonstrate. An incorrect demonstration could lead to students making similar errors, so images/ videos can be useful to ensure students are given the correct information.

There are also a vast number of coaching books which are very useful. These again are sport-specific, but can give very detailed technical knowledge to help you understand common errors within practical skills.

Some books also contain a wide range of drills which can be used within your teaching. These can be very useful if you are struggling to plan a number of activities to develop a particular skill within a sport.

Observing others

One of the most useful resource within a department is the staff you are working with.

It does not matter what stage of their career they are at, they will always have a range of ideas, practices and knowledge which you can learn from.

Here are some tips to help you when going to observe someone else teach:

- Make sure you have approached the teacher prior to the observation to make sure they are happy with you watching their lesson.

- Find out the context of the lesson: What activity are they teaching? What is the focus of the lesson? What are they expecting the students to achieve by the end?

- Ask for a little bit of information regarding the students: Any behavioural issues? Special educational needs? What is the ability of the class?

- Decide on a focus for your observation. Are you observing to learn new ideas about teaching a specific skill, or gaining insight on how to manage students in a practical environment?

The focus is up to you, but highlighting this prior to the observation will allow you to reflect afterwards, rather than it just becoming a general observation of someone teaching.

- Following the observation, discuss what you have seen with the teacher. Try to understand why they have done certain things you have seen, or discuss how you may be able to apply what you have seen to your own lessons.

  Try to keep a record of your observations. This will be an expectation when you start your teaching training, so it is a good habit to get in to.

  However, it also allows you to document what you have seen, allowing you to revisit it when you are due to teach a similar topic, or are faced with a similar situation to the one you observed.

It is worth observing as much teaching as you can before you start your teacher training course. It will give you valuable insights about the role, as well as giving you a range of ideas to apply into your own lesson planning.

While in your training year, and within your first teaching year, you will be given additional time which you can use to help your development. Try to use this time to observe your colleagues and continually learn new approaches you can trial yourself.

Another consideration is observing teachers of subjects other than PE. This is particularly useful if you have not experienced teaching within a classroom environment. But can also be useful to improve your teaching skills, such as developing your questioning, or how to adapt written tasks when students need additional support.

Utilising your most-able students

There may be times that you are faced with students within your class that may know more about certain activities than you do, so why not utilise these students within your teaching?

If you were to have a student who is performing at a national standard in a given activity, are you really going to be expected to stretch this student in relation to the sport?

Empowering these sporting experts to develop and lead small practices, coach other students, or contribute to your planning are different methods which will have two possible outcomes:

1. Improve your subject knowledge within that sport/activity, or contribute to the delivery of certain components of the lesson.

2. Stretch the student by applying their sporting knowledge within different roles and responsibilities.

You must take care when using this approach to ensure that the highly able student is still being involved in a learning experience. Combining this with the ideas presented in Chapter 6: *Providing for the most able within PE*, will ensure they are still making progress, not within the taught activity, but within different inter-personal skills, such as leadership.

There is also a danger of this approach being overused, which may lead to some behavioural difficulties – so be sure to use it in moderation.

It is important to realise that it does not make you an inadequate teacher if a student knows more than you about a particular activity. What it does present, however, is an opportunity to develop your knowledge from a different source.

Community club links

One of the key aims of PE and school sport is to increase the transition from students doing physical activity within their school day, to continuing to perform within a community sport setting.

These community sport providers have an invested interest in linking with local schools – so the more they can work with you, the higher the chance of your students joining their club.

Improving subject knowledge

Community club coaches or volunteers may be willing to visit your school, and provide some of their sporting knowledge to you and you students. There are a number of ways this can happen:

- *Contribution within lessons*: It may be the case that certain coaches would be happy to deliver some sessions within curriculum PE time.

  This is not a provision to 'free-up' a member of teaching staff, but an opportunity to work alongside a teacher to share new ideas and practices.

  Ideas gained in these lessons could be easily replicated or adapted to other teaching groups, aiding your lesson planning.

  This also allows students to get to know a community club coach, which may give some students the confidence to visit the club once they know someone who will be coaching there.

- *Extra-curricular clubs*: It may not be possible for a community coach to visit your school during the school day due to their own commitments. If they are available outside of these times, it may be possible that they can contribute to a departments extra-curricular activities.

  As above, it is important that the coaches are not delivering these sessions independently, but working with a member of the PE department. This will have the same advantages as contributing in lessons.

- *Taster sessions*: Some community clubs/coaches will be unable to commit to significant amounts of time throughout the school year. One-off sessions can also be used to the same effect as the two methods already mentioned.

  If the club coaches were to be invited in to your school to deliver a session which was pre-agreed prior to the visit, the same outcomes will occur.

  This could be aimed at an area of the activity you would like support with, or are less-confident delivering as highlighted in your self-assessment.

It is important in this context to ensure the coach has adequate information about the students they will be working with, and the ability they are so that they can plan the activities appropriately.

- *Gifted and Talented workshops*: As previously discussed, it can be difficult to challenge a student within an activity you are less knowledgeable about, or that they already perform at a high standard.

  Inviting community coaches to deliver some sessions aimed at your most able will provide you with some ideas which would help you to cater for other more-able students in your future planning.

- *Coaching development*: Some larger clubs may provide their own coaching development workshops. It is worth investigating this as these tend to be very effective ways of improving sport-specific knowledge.

  Again, it is within the best interests of the club to develop the knowledge of the local PE teachers, to contribute to the successful delivery of the sport within the area.

  They are also significantly cheaper when compared to official courses from sports providers.

Continuing Professional Development (CPD)

CPD is a commonly-used term within teaching, and refers to all of the things we can do to improve our teaching.

As you start your teacher training, you will need to highlight the areas you wish to develop, and put plans in place to address your needs. This process will continue throughout your career, and will eventually act as part of an appraisal process – which could influence your salary or development needs in the future.

It is important to continue to self-assess your needs throughout your career, and continue to develop your ideas, and knowledge to adapt to the needs of different students you may be faced with.

169

CHAPTER SUMMARY

- Poor subject knowledge is one of the most common concerns for trainee teachers.
- Self-assess your needs, and start to plan strategies to address any gaps in your knowledge.
- Look at the subject as a whole, you will need to feel confident and competent to teach a wide range of activities.
- Familiarise yourself with the resources readily available to you, particularly when planning to teach a unit of work.
- Create opportunities to observe others; gain new ideas, insights and practices which you can replicate or develop within your own planning.
- Continue to analyse your subject knowledge throughout your career, addressing your needs and developing your knowledge wherever possible.

TALKING POINTS

1. How could poor subject knowledge negatively affect your teaching?
2. What topics would you consider to be your weakest? And how can you address these?
3. What are the advantages of observing teachers outside of your subject?
4. How can you use observations to improve your own teaching?

14 Health and safety in PE

Whether you are a qualified teacher, or an additional adult within an education setting, you will have a responsibility to manage the health and safety aspects for the students in your care.

Physical Education and sport both present a number of risks and safety factors which will need to be managed appropriately – this is part of what makes our subject unique.

But who is solely responsible for the health and safety of students within your classes?

Until you are a qualified teacher, the legal responsibility remains with the qualified teacher in charge of the class. For this reason, you must always ensure that you are not left alone with a class prior to, or during your teaching training period.

Although you will not hold the legal responsibility, you will still be required to manage the health and safety factors associated with teaching.

This chapter will outline some of the processes you can go through to ensure your lessons and activities are safe.

Following health and safety guidance/ legislation

Within every PE department, and every school, there are certain policies which are available to you to support anything related to health and safety.

Health and safety in PE

One of the more useful documents is 'Safe Practice in Physical Education, School Sport and Physical Activity'. This document has been produced, and updated to give you knowledge of how to keep students and yourself safe within PE.

This document is produced by, and available from The Association for Physical Education (AfPE), and is accompanied with regular updates to ensure your health and safety protocols remain up-to-date.

Once you begin working in a school, it is important that one of your first tasks is to find out who at the school is responsible for health and safety. The person is usually titled: 'Health and safety officer'.

This person will be useful to you if you require any advice or support while working within the school. It is, however, unlikely that this person has a PE background, so it can be just as useful to ask colleagues within the PE department if you have any questions/ concerns.

There should also be a health and safety policy within the PE department for you to make reference to. This will include information such as:

- Location of first aid kits
- A detailed list of each first aid kits content
- List of qualified first aiders
- What you should do if someone becomes ill/injured during a PE lesson
- Outline of the protocol for injuries when working off-site, such as trips and sports fixtures
- Details of what is required of you after an incident/injury within a lesson (usually completion of a record to document what has happened).

It is not expected that you memorise this policy as soon as you start working within the school, but it is there for you to use when needed.

Teaching students to manage safety

Although you as the teacher have the sole responsibility for health and safety, do we not have a duty to teach our students how to manage their own risks within PE lessons?

This is an important part of Physical Education, and should be built into our lessons to ensure students continually assess risks, and minimise the likelihood of any accidents which could result in an injury.

As you begin your lesson planning, the first element of practical activity will be a warm up – an activity which is consistently in place for two reasons:

1. To create a safe environment, and reduce the risk of any physical injuries.

2. To teach our students how to effectively prepare for physical activity.

Ideally, we should expect our students to do these warm-ups independently – but this is an expectation you may need to develop over time.

Students should be taught, and given opportunities to make decisions about how to adequately prepare for any activities they will be performing within their lessons. And this will need to be supervised by you as the teacher.

But why not take this further – could our students be involved in assessing risks which may be present throughout their lessons?

Asking your class questions about safety and risk factors can be a very effective way of highlighting these to the students, without just presenting the students with this information.

For example, consider teaching a rugby lesson focusing on tackling. By asking students what they feel may be the risks associated with this skill, or activities they are about to perform should highlight any risks associated and therefore you are fulfilling your role.

Or consider a gymnastics activity which uses pieces of apparatus. Is there any reason why students should not be involved in deciding where this equipment can be safely placed within the teaching space?

A similar range of questions as in the above rugby tackling example, will also allow students to assess any risks linked to using the apparatus, and reduce the chances of them being misused.

These examples do not mean you are giving the students the responsibility of making your lessons safe.

You are involving them in the process of making your lesson safe and teaching them appropriate health and safety information in the process.

Risk assessments

These are procedures which are put in place to highlight any potential risks, and implementing methods to reduce the probability of these risks occurring.

You do not need to produce a formal risk assessment for every lesson you are due to teach, but you will need to include elements of this process within your planning.

Risk assessments must be produced if you are taking students off-site, for example a school trip. But what does a risk assessment actually include?

There are a number of different formats which are readily available on the internet, or can be given to you by your school's health and safety officer.

By adhering to the following steps, you will be covering the expected criteria of a risk assessment. An example for each step has been included for gymnastics:

1.   **Identifying the hazards**: Assess your teaching area. Is there anything present which could cause an accident or injury to a student?

Example: When planning a gymnastics lesson, any apparatus being used could have a risk associated.

Consider a standard gym bench – this equipment allows students to work at height, therefore a certain amount of risk can be associated.

2. **Who may be harmed, and how could they be harmed?** Can you be harmed as the teacher? Can students be harmed when using this equipment? Or when setting up certain items of apparatus?

Once this information has been ascertained, you will need to outline how someone could be harmed.

Example: Is it possible to be harmed when moving a gym bench? The answer to this should be yes.

Outlining how this could occur may include moving a bench individually, or a student dropping the bench while moving it.

3. **How much of a risk is present?** This requires you to assess the probability of this risk occurring.

There are a number of ways this can be completed, and different styles of risk assessment may require different things.

A typical risk assessment would include categorizing the risk in to one of three levels: low, moderate and high.

Example: For the example of moving the gym bench, the risk would be categorized as low.

A moderate to high risk during a gymnastics lesson could be when you first start to teach more complex skills, such as vaulting, which require students to be working at speed and height.

4. **What existing procedures are in place to reduce the chance of the risk causing harm?** This will require you to outline what precautions are already in place, if any, to reduce the chance of this risk occurring.

Example: This could be as simple as clear verbal instructions being given prior to anyone moving the gym bench.

Or could be protocols such as safety posters, or demonstrations giving everyone sufficient knowledge on how to move the equipment safely.

5. **Is there anything else which could be put into place to decrease the chance of causing harm more?** This will require you to review the last stage of the process, and highlight if any more could be done to increase the safety of your lesson.

Example: In this example, it could be argued that no more actions would be required to make this process safer.

6. **Review the assessment/amend your assessment**: Has the precaution which was put in place been successful? Have any accidents/injuries occurred since this procedure was put into place?

Example: If no instances of accidents or injuries occur, there may not be a need to change anything.

It is however, still important to review your procedures, and adapt precautions in relation to the class you are teaching.

Lifting instructions that you give to the class may differ between a Year 7 class, and a Year 11 group. You will need to make that judgement and ensure your instructions are effective.

A risk assessment for sports fixtures will be a general one covering all sports fixtures for the department.

Inductions

Teaching students to use equipment properly and safely is an important part of your role.

Formalizing these instructions can be an effective way of ensuring equipment and facilities are used correctly.

This is in line with the expectation of an adult joining their local gym.

If students are going to be given access to fitness equipment, or free weights, there will be elements of risk present. Guiding students through an induction session would be necessary to ensure they have the appropriate knowledge to use the facility safely.

An effective induction session should include step-by-step instructions, describing how it should be used correctly. This involves describing correct techniques, and warnings if using equipment which could put large amounts of stress on the students.

Example: Describing the appropriate use of the 'leg press' machine.

1. Check the weight is appropriate for you, and change if necessary.

2. Take care when changing the weights to avoid trapping your fingers.

3. Check the angle/height of the seat is appropriate for your size.

4. Place soles of feet flat against the foot-plate, with your feet shoulder-distance apart.

5. Extend legs slowly, but make sure they are not fully extended to avoid putting pressure on the joint (do not 'lock' your knees).

6. Slowly return to starting position.

It is important to demonstrate the appropriate technique to ensure all of the students understand your instructions. It is also powerful to involve students in the demonstration to reinforce the steps you have described.

As with your local gym, it may also be important for students to be 'signed off', which demonstrates they can use the equipment appropriately and safely.

Safety checks

This is similar to the protocol outlined within the risk assessment method earlier within this chapter.

Any facility or equipment you chose to use within your lesson will need to be checked.

Some equipment will not need checking every lesson, but periodic checks will be important, for example ensuring any basketball hoops attached to walls are safe to use.

Facility checks will need to happen at the start of the lesson. This will include checking to see if there are any water spillages on a sports hall floor. Or are there any 'pot-holes' present on your playing field.

Again, this part of the safety process could be completed by students effectively, and your pupils will need to learn how to complete this process as part of their knowledge to exercise safely.

Weather

This variable is one we have very little control over. But at what stage does the weather create an unsafe environment?

As a general rule, most schools will try to continue with their PE lesson despite the weather as long as the lesson remains safe.

There may be instances that your lesson will need to be adapted to cope with weather conditions.

In cold temperatures, it is important to ensure that the class remains active for long periods so you may need to reduce the amount of time they are standing still.

It may be appropriate to spend some extended time indoors, such as some group discussion tasks inside the changing rooms, to decrease the amount of time the students will need to be outside.

If this is a method you are going to use, be sure you have some activities planned linked to your lesson objective to ensure you do not encounter any behavioural issues.

Tactical discussions, application of tactics within scenarios, or linking the unit of work with some theoretical concepts are examples of some of the tasks you could implement.

There will be times where this is not possible. When temperatures drop below freezing, when rainfall floods the playing area and at times when the temperature is too high.

You will need to make a professional judgement about whether to continue with your lesson outside when the weather may be a concern – but you must always ensure that the lesson remains safe.

Consider if the students are dressed appropriately, and whether your activity can be adapted effectively to deal with the adverse weather.

Off-site activities

Any activities that occur off-site are accompanied with different risks and considerations you will need to make.

The most common off-site activities for a PE teacher will be sports fixtures. But what considerations do you need to make to ensure that your students are safe while visiting another school/ facility?

Firstly, you will need to inform the appropriate people within your school about the students you wish to take off-site.

Each school will have a slightly different routine to do this, but it may be as simple as handing a list of student names to your school's reception.

It is important the school is aware of all of the students you will be with in case a parent contacts the school in an emergency.

Parents will also need to be informed that you are taking their child away from the school site.

Some schools will have a policy in which parents will need to sign a reply slip to give permission, other schools will send an email to parents to inform them – this will be dependent on your school/department.

You will then need to ensure you take with you the emergency contact details for the students you are travelling with. Good examples of this will also include medical/dietary requirements to support you if needed.

For the event/fixture, you will need to make sure that you carry a first aid kit with you at all times. Small first aid kits, in a backpack are ideal for sports fixtures/events.

A mobile phone to contact your school, or any parents if there is a need to will also be important.

Your school should have a generic risk assessment for off-site activities, such as fixtures so you will not need to complete one of these for every fixture you take.

However, some sports fixtures may require more than one person to be present, and this is usually based on a teacher-to-student ratio.

There are some activities that have a higher risk element which may also be worth considering an additional member of staff to accompany the event, such as contact rugby.

Also, remember that until you are a qualified teacher, it is important that you are not left alone with any group without the presence of another member of staff.

Additional safety equipment

There are also a number of items which can be used to increase the safety of some activities; some are compulsory and others are highly recommended.

Below are the most common items of safety equipment/clothing for traditional PE activities:

- **Shin pads**: These are compulsory items for football and hockey.

- **Gum shields**: These are highly recommended for contact rugby, hockey and other contact activities. Some schools will state these are compulsory.

- **Protective headwear**: Some activities make this a compulsory item. For example, when playing cricket, you must wear a helmet while batting.

  You may also be teaching more alternative activities, such as cycling, which will also require specialist protective headwear.

- **Studded footwear**: These tend to not be compulsory, but some activities will become unsafe without them.

  If teaching rugby on soft, wet ground, studded footwear is very important, particularly if the students are learning to ruck, maul or take part in scrums.

- **Post protectors**: Important for sports where collisions with goal posts is a potential risk. These are compulsory for competitive rugby matches.

There are many other items which can be used to create a safer environment, but some may come at a significant financial cost.

It is important to remember that PE and school sport creates a certain amount of risk to students. We can control these risks to some extent, but the very nature of some of the activities we teach may result in injuries or accidents.

As long as protocols are in place to reduce the risks of harming our students, and safety concerns have been considered in your planning, you can be confident that your lessons are being conducted within a safe environment.

CHAPTER SUMMARY

- You are responsible for ensuring that your lessons are safe for all students.
- Know where to access any department/school policies regarding health and safety.
- Make yourself familiar with the school's nominated health and safety officer, and seek advice from them (or a member of your department) if you require it for your planning.
- Take steps to ensure your lessons are safe; risk assessments, equipment and safety checks are an important part of your lesson preparation.
- Teach your students to be involved with the health and safety considerations.
- You will need to make professional judgements in some situations and decide whether your lesson is safe to take place in extreme cases of bad weather.
- Know what safety equipment is compulsory, highly recommended or available for the activities you are due to teach.

TALKING POINTS

1. How can you effectively involve students when conducting risk assessments?
2. When teaching outdoors, at what point does adverse weather deem your lesson to be unsafe?
3. When teaching activities where safety equipment is strongly recommended (e.g. rugby), how would you act if a number of your students did not have the equipment for your lesson?
4. What steps would you take before taking students off-site?

15 From PE to community sport

One of the key aims of Physical Education is to educate students to make effective decisions regarding their health and well-being.

These decisions may include students participating in physical activity, or sport, outside of curriculum PE.

What can we do as PE teachers to increase the probability of our students actively participating in sport and physical activity outside of school?

There are a number of effective strategies you can use to accomplish this. The approaches below are not an exhaustive list, but will provide some important factors for you to consider.

The concept of lifelong learning

This idea centres around our teaching including skills and knowledge which students can use voluntarily beyond their education.

In order for students to be self-motivated to engage in physical activity beyond the classroom, they will need to understand the long-term effects that exercise has on our health. This may include:

- Improving stamina
- Increasing flexibility/strength/suppleness
- Improving core strength (influencing balance)

- Decreasing fat levels/cholesterol
- Reducing chances of diseases (such as heart disease)
- Reducing chances of injuries, or joint pains.

It is important that students understand these effects as it will influence their decision making.

Lifelong learning in PE will also include the development of physical skills. As with physical literacy (previously mentioned in Chapter 17: *The aims of Physical Education*), students will need to acquire certain skills which can then be applied to sport-specific skills.

In relation to physical skills, we have a responsibility to ensure that students leave education with the appropriate fitness to meet the demands of their environment.

That could be the required levels of fitness to complete a shift in a physically demanding occupation, or the fitness and knowledge required to complete their own session in their local gym.

But how much fitness do students require before leaving school?

It is important that students can sustain moderate to vigorous physical activity for a sustained period of time (up to 60 minutes). This will provide an important benchmark for you to work towards.

Another important factor to consider is activities that strengthen our muscles and bones. This could include activities such as cycling, swimming or long-distance running.

Young people are expected to be able to conduct these at least three times per week.

Once a physical capacity has been obtained by the students, they will be able to engage in sports which meet their needs and preference.

As discussed in Chapter 2: *Curriculum essentials in Physical Education*, it is important to ensure students are subjected to a broad 'diet' of activities.

This will have two effects: it will ensure that the students have a wider range of sport-specific skills, which will increase their confidence within more activities. It will also increase the probability of them finding an activity they will enjoy pursuing independently.

Therefore, you will need to consider including a wide range of activities within your curriculum:

• Invasion games, for example football and netball
• Net/wall games, for example badminton and tennis
• Communicating ideas/concepts, for example dance and gymnastics
• Replicating actions, for example trampolining and aerobics
• Health/fitness, for example using a fitness suite and yoga
• Strike and field games, for example cricket and rounders
• Performing at maximum capacity, for example athletics.

With teachers being empowered to make these decisions, it has become more common for more 'modern' activities being included within PE curriculums.

Activities such as skateboarding, BMXing and dodgeball can be included within your curriculum if you see these activities as being more effective with the class you are teaching, and if you can still meet the aims of the curriculum (refer to Chapter 1: *The aims of Physical Education*).

Please remember that to teach these alternative activities safely and effectively, you will need to ensure that you have obtained sufficient subject knowledge, and have the appropriate equipment, facilities and safety precautions in place prior to teaching the activity.

Addressing the post-16 decrease in physical activity

The 'post-16' decrease in physical activity refers to the common trend which occurs following students leaving school in Year 11.

There are a number of factors which can be described as possible causes for this decreased participation in physical activity, these include:

From PE to community sport

- **Increase focus on academic studies**: With a number of students advancing to A levels, or vocational courses, you will see a shift in a student's focus.

  These courses are demanding, and require high levels of self-initiated study outside of lessons, and can at times be to the determent of physical activity.

  This is also compounded by the increased accountability of the students, particularly those who require specific results to access university courses.

- **Part-time employment**: Another common trend as students move into further education is the percentage of students that have part-time employment.

  This can be an important consideration for students, as some will be saving money for university, saving for driving lessons, or contributing to the costs of their studies.

- **Lack of confidence**: It may be that the students have not acquired sufficient skills and abilities to confidently access sport independently.

  Following adolescence, it is common to see students decrease in self-esteem. This is much more prevalent within females, but still affects males.

  Sometimes this can be attributed to a lack in social skills as many of these opportunities will take place with different people, unknown by the student, or within different environments.

- **Disengagement in PE/sport**: If a PE curriculum has been unsuccessful, there may be an increase in disengagement in physical activity.

  This is most common within Key Stage 4 PE lessons, when the students begin to focus on their GCSE studies and may start to perceive PE negatively, or as a waste of their time.

  If the PE curriculum is not perceived as purposeful, or enjoyable, it is bound to have a knock-on effect on a student's engagement in physical activity beyond their education.

- **Financial constraints**: Money can have a significant effect on participation following students leaving the secondary school environment.

  A number of students will become financially independent, and some physical activities can be expensive – such as gym memberships.

Now that we have explored some of the potential factors which could cause the post-16 decrease in participation, what can we do to reduce the drop-out rates within physical activity?

Possible solution 1: Bespoke extra-curricular provision for post-16 students

Within schools that have a Sixth Form College attached, it may be appropriate to devise a bespoke extra-curricular timetable for students within Years 12 and 13.

These students tend to like opportunities that are separate to the rest of the school, making them feel different, and more like young adults than students of the school – consider some additional activities which you could include in your extra-curricular offer to target this age group.

Providing these activities during a lunchtime, or within the school day will remove some of the barriers discussed earlier within this chapter.

As with any extra-curricular timetable, it will be important to include a mixture of competitive and non-competitive activities.

With the competitive activities, you will need to plan potential fixtures or competitions to ensure you maintain engagement for a longer period of time.

Possible solution 2: Participation audit

Consider a short questionnaire which can be given to all students within this age group.

How many of them are currently active? What activities would be effective? What days/times are most appropriate?

This information is vital if you are planning an extra-curricular provision that is going to be effective.

Better examples of this would also utilise a group of the students themselves, like a school council group. This would involve the students in the decision process, which would definitely be an advantage when promoting the activities to the rest of the students.

Possible solution 3: Inter-school competitions

As stated earlier in this chapter, participation in competitive activities will need some sort of 'exit route' to ensure the students remain engaged for a longer period of time.

If your school has a 'house system' in place, where students are already divided, providing some regular sporting competitions could prove effective.

Consider including activities that can be participated by both genders at the same time, such as basketball and rounders, which will also reduce the effects of lower self-esteem displayed by some females.

Possible solution 4: Alternative activities

There may be an opportunity to offer some alternative activities which are not on the school's PE curriculum.

More recreational activities such as informal badminton sessions can be effective, but may only attract students which are already engaged.

Why not consider some activities that are slightly different, such as zorb football or archery – which may require additional funding, but would provide a unique opportunity which may improve engagement.

It is common for students to acquire gym memberships beyond leaving school – is there anything within these environments they are offered which you can use?

Yoga sessions, Zumba classes or fitness boot camps may be worth exploring.

Possible solution 5: One-off conference style event

Devising a solution that is different can be very effective. A conference-style event focused around health and well-being could be planned to try to engage students in a range of different activities.

These activities can all be related to improving health and wellbeing, tackling mental health issues, as well as inactivity levels.

Workshop ideas could include:

- Yoga
- Pilates
- Massage
- Healthy eating
- Self-defence
- Zumba.

Allowing students to opt for different physical activities throughout the day would subject them to a number of different activities – which may also provide you with an insight into which activities would be most effective when tackling inactivity.

This type of event may require additional staffing, but it is worth inquiring with local health providers as they may want to be involved to promote their own organisations.

Transition from PE to school sport

If we want to encourage our students to independently engage with competitive sports, we will need to provide some competitive opportunities in order to build their confidence.

This initially will be included within PE lessons, but will then need to be developed further through school sports teams.

This may also present an opportunity for you to encourage certain students to attend the school sports club to extend their knowledge. This could be students who display a good ability within lessons who you feel may benefit from extending their skills/knowledge, or could be inviting targeted individuals that are currently not active in school sport.

Leagues and tournaments are produced and organised for schools to compete in. Your role will be to organise the dates and times of the fixture(s), and choose the team of students you wish to compete.

Allowing students interested in competing to attend training sessions each week will allow you to further extend their skills beyond what is included within their curriculum PE lessons.

If there is no provision in your local area for the sports club you have organised, there is no reason why you could not plan your own fixtures or competitions by contacting your local schools.

Transition from school sport to community sport

The next step following a student's participation in a school sports team, will be for the student to progress towards participating in a community sports team.

For this to happen, you may need to direct students towards their local opportunities.

Contact details for local coaches, or timings of training sessions open for them to attend will be important information.

Some schools will have a dedicated display space around their changing room areas which has this information readily available for students to access.

Involvement in a community club will prove a very effective way to sustain the students interest in the sport. It will also provide them with extended knowledge of the sport, and potential to compete at a higher standard.

School–club links

There are a number of ways to increase the probability of students engaging with community sports clubs.

Any link you can establish with a local sports club, or local coaches will increase the likelihood of students transferring to the community club setting.

Allowing the community coaches to contribute to your PE curriculum is an effective way to do this. This could be by inviting the coaches to deliver sessions within your PE curriculum, or supporting an extra-curricular club.

Some local clubs may be happy to promote themselves in school assemblies, or give you some promotional material to give to your students.

Another way to improve the link between the school and community sports club is via a programme called 'satellite clubs'.

Satellite clubs are extensions of community clubs which are established within the secondary school environment via funding from Sport England.

For satellite clubs to be successful, there must be an appropriate need in your area for the club to be established: Is there another local club that is accessible to your students? Or would this club significantly increase participation in sport for your students?

These are particularly useful to engage students who may not be confident in engaging with a club in a new environment.

Additional opportunities to increase engagement with community clubs

It is important to remember that some students may not want to participate in competitive sport or recreational activities.

What else can be available to these students to increase their engagement with your local community, and increase their participation?

Leadership, coaching and volunteering opportunities can be a very effective way to do this.

Creating opportunities for your students to work with community sports clubs or local organisations to support events, or officiate competitions are just two examples of how you can apply this to your students.

For this to be effective, you will need to ensure that the students have an adequate skill set to be successful in this environment, or direct them towards the appropriate training for them to do this independently.

CHAPTER SUMMARY

- A key aim of Physical Education is to educate students to make effective decisions regarding their health and well-being.
- It is important to ensure that we consider lifelong learning objectives which allow our students to participate in physical activity beyond their education.
- One of the most common decreases in physical activity occurs with students as they turn 16 years old – what can you do within your school to address this?
- Consider the range of activities which are available to your students to maximise the probability of the students transferring into a community club setting.
- Utilise local sports clubs and coaches within your curriculum and extra-curricular offer.
- Some students may benefit from engaging with a community partner within a different capacity, such as volunteering.

TALKING POINTS

1. What can you do within lessons to decrease inactivity levels outside of school?
2. Are there any alternative activities you can include within your extra-curricular offer to increase participation?
3. What local sports coaches could you utilise within your school/department?
4. How can you increase the number of students that transition into a community club setting within PE lessons?

16 Job applications and interview advice

The initial year of teacher training brings with it many challenges: the stresses of planning and assessing, completing assignments, compiling a portfolio of evidence and the list goes on . . .

Added to that, from the end of your first term in the training year, you will need to focus on your future, and start making decisions about where to apply your trade.

The application and interview process for teaching is a very unique and intense process. The duration from when the post is first advertised to an appointment being made is very short – and will include many components which will now be explored.

This chapter will walk you through the entire process of seeking your first teaching post, from where to look for vacancies to the end of your interview day. This can be categorised into two sections: The application process and the interview process.

The application process

- Searching for teaching posts
- Writing application forms
- Covering letters/personal statements.

Searching for teaching posts

One of the benefits of teacher training is the fact that you would have gained experience in more than one school. Placements are usually carefully selected to ensure your training incorporates two contrasting experiences.

This aims to develop your skills in different contexts, and provide you with the necessary experiences to make an informed decision about the kind of establishment you would like to start your career.

The teaching experience varies within every school you work in and is dependent on many variables: size of the school, number of students on roll, facilities, volume of support staff, reputation and geographical location to name a few.

Therefore, it is important to not 'jump' towards the first teaching post that is advertised, but to consider what type of school would give you the best foundations in which to start your career.

One of the most effective ways to find out about teaching posts available is via your training provider. They will have constant contact with a large number of schools, and are usually contacted when posts suitable for newly-qualified teachers become available.

There are many websites that continually advertise teaching posts, such as the TES. One of the most effective ways to use these sites is to set up email alerts for the type of role you are looking for (e.g. secondary, Physical Education).

One of the unique features of a PE teacher is the regular contact we have with colleagues from different schools – fixtures, local area PE meetings, competitions and events are all ways in which PE staff congregate on a fairly regular basis. Use these to begin networking, making good impressions and showing interest in any posts which may become available.

Writing application forms

The written application form will differ from school to school, but will contain some consistent elements.

This is a key component of the process as it will determine whether or not you will be invited to attend an interview. PE posts are currently very popular, and there is a large number of teachers that wish to work within our subject.

Therefore, it is important to ensure that your application makes you 'stand out' from the other applicants, and conforms to the needs and requirements of the department/school you are applying to join.

Covering letters/personal statements

One consistent element of this process is the personal statement. This can sometimes be submitted as a 'covering letter', but there is no need to do both.

It is important to ensure your personal statement is interesting – you want whomever is reading it to be interested with your application, and to be perceived as someone who will make a significant impact if employed.

Be careful not to re-write information which may be present elsewhere in the application. For example, long lists of coaching qualifications are a great way to highlight your subject knowledge – but not an effective way of enticing a reader.

Consider content that will set you apart from the other applicants. It is important to draw upon your previous experiences, this could be things you have done prior to your training year – but must be relevant to the teaching post, and used to inform the reader of what you can offer their school.

Before writing your personal statement, it is important that you do two things: re-read the job description, and visit the school's website.

The job description should inform you of some of the key characteristics that the school/department are looking for. For example, will the post involve teaching examination elements of the subject (e.g. GCSE, A-Level, or BTEC). If so, it would be worth including some information about your ability to teach these, and what you could bring to the role.

Sometimes a teaching post can include requirements to take a leading role in certain activities. For example, is the school looking for someone to contribute to their rugby or hockey extra-curricular provision?

In relation to the school website, reading through the school's 'mission statement' can be an effective way to plan the context of your statement.

For example, if the school has a particular focus on developing literacy, how can you contribute to this within the role of a PE teacher? Maybe the school has a distinctive focus on developing student leadership, what can you bring to this element of the school?

These elements are important as it shows the reader that you know about the school, and it highlights your desire to join their team of teaching staff.

Finally, once you have completed your personal statement, proof-read it. Then proof-read it again, and ask someone else to read it for you too. This sounds patronising, but it can be the difference between yourself and other applicants. Typos, spelling errors and incorrect information will lead the reader to believe you have either rushed your application, or show little interest in the position.

Once this has been completed, ensure the application is submitted by the deadline. Most teaching vacancies include an interview date or the week of the interview. You will be contacted if your application is successful with more information about the interview process.

The interview process

- Prior visit
- Pre-interview info
- Tour

- Student panel
- Written task
- Teaching session
- Post-interview.

Prior visit

It is difficult to determine whether a school is right for you without seeing it first-hand. A visit prior to you submitting your application can be an effective way to counter this.

This part of the process is not essential – the teaching post you are applying for may be abroad, or too far away to travel to for an informal visit. Not visiting prior to applying will not count against you.

The visit presents an opportunity to 'put a face to the name' in relation to your written application, plus providing additional opportunities to determine what characteristics the school are looking for and to make a good impression.

If you do decide to visit the school, be sure to ask lots questions to gain an insight into the school, the department and the requirements of the advertised post.

Pre-interview information

If your application has been successful, you will be contacted by the school to attend the interview. At this point, the school will provide you with some information regarding the day.

Date, times and location are the obvious inclusions in this information, but you will also be provided with some of the content of the day. Typically, this will include a tour of the school, a teaching session and a formal interview.

As a PE teacher, if you are due to be teaching a practical session you will require your sports attire. Take this with you to the interview and change before your teaching – remember at this stage you are making immediate impressions about yourself.

School tour

If you were not able to visit the school prior to the interview, this is a great opportunity to gain an insight into the day-to-day running of the establishment.

As a PE teacher, it is important to see the facilities that will be available to you if you are successful.

You will also gain an understanding of variables such as students' behaviour, may get the opportunity to briefly visit lessons and are bound to meet potential future colleagues.

It is important to remember that this is still part of the interview process. Although it is one of the less formal elements, people are still making initial judgements of you to ensure they make an effective appointment.

Be sure to ask lots questions about the school, engage with other staff while being shown around the site and be confident.

Student panel

It is becoming more common to see students involved in the interview process. It could be that some students have taken you on the school tour, but they will still be asked for feedback which will contribute to the employment decision.

A student panel, or student interview can be a very powerful way to gauge how you can foster the interest of young people.

Students are also experts in what characteristics create a good teacher, and can devise some interesting questions for you to answer.

They will know that the best teachers in their school are those with high expectations of them, have clear boundaries and take an interest in their progress. It is worth considering how you can get this message across to young people.

The important part of this phase of any interview is to sustain purposeful and interesting dialogue with the students. It is also another opportunity for you to ask some questions, and students are generally very honest with their responses.

Written task

These can vary from school-to-school, and the rationale behind the task will inform how you should complete it.

It is possible that you may be asked to complete some example examination questions. This will aim to assess your subject knowledge, while also highlighting your use of appropriate terminology, spelling and use of language.

Applicants with additional needs, such as dyslexia, would need to inform the school of this prior to the interview to ensure the task can still be completed. This will not count against you.

Other tasks may include analysing data, planning a competition/event/task or responding to a relevant sport-specific news article.

Remember that although you are applying for a teaching post in PE, you will still have a responsibility to develop students' literacy and use of language, which is what this element aims to determine.

Teaching session

This is usually the component that most interviewees worry about. We are all passionate about our teaching, and want every lesson we teach to be deemed 'outstanding' – but this is your chance to show you can do it.

If you have not been supplied with sufficient information regarding the teaching session – ask before the day. This can include:

- Number of students in the class
- Gender of students
- Age
- Ability
- Special educational needs
- English as an additional language.

This is not the only information you will need to exchange. If you have not visited the school, do you know the size of the facility you will have to teach in? Are there any items of equipment you need for your lesson?

It is important that all of this information is exchanged prior to the interview to ensure you can plan your session accordingly.

The actual teaching session itself will bring a different challenge. You will not know the students you are teaching so may have to adapt the activities you have planned accordingly.

Don't be afraid to change activities during your lesson. It will not be seen negatively, but will show your ability to reflect during a lesson and adapt in accordance to students' needs.

A common trend with interview lessons is to plan a basic, straight forward lesson – which you know will go well with few problems and will show your ability to teach.

However, remember that you are in competition with other potential candidates – do things that will make your lesson stand out, but ensure you have the basics right:

- High expectations
- Clear instructions
- Demonstrate student progress
- Consider health and safety
- Include the 'nuts-and-bolts' which contribute to a good lesson (e.g. starter/plenary).

If your lesson is practical, try to avoid long periods of time where the students are static. It is important to have a quick start to the lesson, and keep the students' active and engaged.

Another pitfall to avoid is excessive teacher-input. It can be very easy to over-explain tasks, answer questions for students and repeat statements when you are nervous.

Remember, a lesson is about students doing (learning), not you as the teacher doing the work for them.

Formal interview

This is generally the last component of the interview. You will be invited individually to answer questions to a panel of staff.

This will usually consist of the Head Teacher, the Head of Department, and a member of staff responsible for student safeguarding.

Try not to answer questions before you have an opportunity to consider your answer, this will lead to you repeating yourself and not answering in a clear and precise manner.

If you need to take a few seconds to think about the question, or if you are unsure what is being asked, be confident and ask the interviewer to re-word or repeat the question.

You will be asked to reflect on your lesson. It is important to be honest, but not over-critical. Suggest ways you would change the lesson if you were to do it again, and highlight components you felt went well.

You may also be asked to elaborate on information present in your application, another good reason to ensure the information you have provided is accurate and thought-provoking.

Post-interview

You will often either be told at the end of the day, or early the next day whether you have been offered the position.

Accepting the position verbally acts as an 'unwritten contract'. Be sure to not change your mind from this point, as it will look extremely unprofessional and may affect future opportunities.

If you are unfortunately unsuccessful, you should be offered the opportunity to receive some feedback on the day – be sure to take the school up on this offer.

It may provide you with some information about what to change in your next interview, highlight what went well and what areas you need to develop.

CHAPTER SUMMARY

- Start looking for your first teaching post from term two of your training year.
- Research the school, department and job in detail to be sure you are making an informed decision about applying for the post – and use this information in your application.
- Take care when completing your written application, and be sure to proof-read everything you are sending to your potential employer.
- Carefully consider your practical teaching session, and include elements which show-off the kind of teacher you are.
- Be sure to highlight what you will bring to the role.

TALKING POINTS

1. What qualities, or provisions, would make a school an attractive place to start your career?
2. What information do you require to effectively plan a lesson for the purposes of an interview?
3. How can you display your skills and qualities to your potential employers within an interview?
4. What questions could be asked to you during a formal interview? And how will you respond to them effectively?

17 Your first term in post

This chapter will explore the various things you are likely to encounter during the first term in post. These will include: workload, behaviour, planning, working with colleagues, additional responsibilities, emotional ups and downs, the transition from training to teaching and dealing with unexpected problems.

This chapter will focus on how to overcome difficulties and how to deal positively with new or difficult situations. We will conclude with some top tips for becoming a great teacher of Physical Education.

From training to teaching

The first difference you will notice is the volume of teaching you will be timetabled for. As a 'newly-qualified teacher' (NQT) you will be given an additional 10% of preparation time compared to other teachers with more than one year's experience.

This extra time is for you to use to help to develop your teaching, and there are a number of ways you can choose to use it.

Watch and learn

Consider watching other colleagues, in and outside of your department. This is invaluable, but unless you schedule in some

204

observations, they will get squeezed out by the frenzy of daily routines.

Try to build-in at least a lesson per month when you watch someone else teach and then talk to them about how they planned, and how they led the lesson. In other words – learn from some of the veterans of the school.

In particular, watch teachers who specialise in various skills and approaches. Watch a teacher of Physics to see how they take complex ideas and make them clear for their students. Watch a teacher of PSHE to look at the use of class discussion. Watch a Drama teacher to see how they organise group and pair work.

This isn't a case of just watching the best teachers. In particular, you might not learn a huge amount by watching a senior teacher whose perfect discipline arises from their long-established reputation, or who teaches through charisma. Teachers like this are great to watch. But it's really important to watch people whose skills you can dissect, analyse and learn from.

You don't have to watch the whole lesson. Watch how a teacher kicks off their teaching, or watch the middle or end of a lesson. Then try to get time to listen to the teacher's own reflections on how the lesson went.

Doing this throughout your career – watching teachers as teachers and also as form tutors – helps build a reflective approach into your own development. It's invaluable.

You will be able to pick up tips and teaching methods from others within the profession, and it can act as a great way to further develop your subject knowledge.

Create resources

This additional time is also useful to create resources that can be easily adapted to groups you will be teaching. Task cards, worksheets and lesson plans take a lot of time to develop, but once in place they can be a valuable resource to use and share.

You should also be allocated a mentor within your new school. You will not need to meet this person on a regular basis, but it is useful to know that there is someone in school you can call upon for support/advice if needed.

There are also many courses available to help develop your teaching. As a PE specialist, there may be a need for you to develop your subject knowledge in certain activity areas.

All major examination boards offer courses to help teachers prepare to teach their subjects at both GCSE and A level. These courses will develop your knowledge and understanding of the specifications, and will also offer practical advice for how to teach certain topics.

One of the most positive factors when starting your first teaching post, is the fact that your classes are now your own and you no longer share groups with their original teacher.

Consider what personal 'tweaks' you can add to your practice. For example, what classroom routines will you enforce as students arrive for their practical lesson at the changing rooms?

Remember that greeting students at the start of the lesson (regardless of it being in the changing rooms rather than the classroom) is very powerful, this is the starting point of your lesson – and the students need to know that.

Students will very quickly pick up your expectations, so consider your teaching style and what to expect from your classes. Do you want the students to warm up independently at the start of your lesson? If the answer is yes, you will need to enforce this at the start so that it becomes automatic.

It is also important to consider your medium and long term planning. Most departments will already have schemes of work to guide you through the expected learning outcomes for your groups. Be sure to use these, but teach the topics in a way which works best for you and your students.

Longer term planning in Physical Education tends to be dictated by facilities. It is worth noting what periods of the school year you are due to be teaching outside – will the weather be a factor that determines what activity you may wish to teach?

Assessment in PE is very unique, and dependent on the course you are teaching. Non-examination Physical Education (or core PE) also requires an assessment – so be sure you understand how/when this assessment takes place.

It is a very good idea to continually assess your groups at every stage of a unit of work. Keeping a class list close to allow you to make notes/assessments following tasks/lessons will be useful when completing the formal assessments or report writing.

Managing workload

One of the key factors which is often negatively discussed by teachers is excessive workload. Therefore, managing your time and workload is very important, and if done effectively can make your job much easier.

Think about your work–life balance. This refers to the volume of work you complete in a typical week, compared to the amount of time you have for your personal life.

What's important is to ensure you do not 'burn out' in the early stages of a term. Consider what work you will have during each half-term, and plan accordingly.

One very useful thing to note is when reports/assessments are due in your planner/diary. This will create additional work which can at times be overlooked, and it is difficult to complete these in addition to your normal workload.

As a PE teacher, you will also need to consider your extra-curricular commitments. How many lunchtimes will you have devoted to a sports club, or school team training? How many evenings a week will you be accompanying a school team to a fixture/competition?

Again, this is all part of your role, so you will need to consider these when planning/organising your time.

In relation to your planning, it is obviously important to ensure you are adequately prepared to teach your lessons. However, planning too far ahead will lead to difficulties within PE.

If your planning exceeds a week in advance, your planned lesson will almost definitely need to change. This could be due to a number of factors, which includes the expected progress of your students, compared to how they progress in reality.

Likewise, you may need to adjust your planning due to extraneous weather variables. A good example of this is with athletics. It is hard to plan what activities you are going to teach too far in advance as some activities are not appropriate in certain weather conditions.

Recall any javelin lesson you may have taught or observed in the past. Would it be appropriate to teach this lesson if the temperatures fall or if the ground surface is wet?

So, it is worth planning for the groups next lesson following their last encounter with you, and ensuring that you do not plan too far in advance.

Additional responsibilities

Every teacher will have a number of additional responsibilities which they will need to complete, but there are some that are unique to our specialism.

Secondary school teachers, regardless of their subject area would need to fulfil the following responsibilities:

• **Tutor**: Sometimes known as a 'form tutor' or 'personal tutor'. Common responsibilities in this role include registrations (outside of normal lessons, for example, at the start of the day), and dealing with any issues before the student attends lessons.

This role is the link between home and school, so communication with parents/guardians is paramount.

The tutor is often also responsible for pastoral support (in the first instance – due to the day-to-day contact) and academic progress (an overview of all the subjects each student is taking).

- **Staff duties**: This differs from school-to-school, but could include a weekly duty which forms part of your working week. The role of staff on duty is to have a presence in an area of the school during times that the students are not in lessons (e.g. before-school, break times and after-school).

As a PE teacher, it would be rare that you have a duty over a lunchtime, or after-school due to our commitments to extra-curricular provisions.

- **Meetings**: These will also form part of your weekly planning. Meetings are relatively regular within schools, and can be in place for numerous purposes: department collaboration, pastoral updates, curriculum reviews or meetings with parents/guardians.

As a PE teacher, there may also be times that you meet fellow colleagues from different schools to discuss fixture dates, competitions or collaborate.

As a specialist in Physical Education, there are also a number of responsibilities that you need to consider, which are unique to our subject:

- **Extra-curricular provision**: It is often written into a PE teachers' contract that there is an expectation that you will contribute to sporting activities outside of curriculum time.

These can be provisions that take place before school, at lunchtimes or after school.

School sports teams will require training sessions, fixtures and/or competitions. But there is also a requirement to ensure you maximize the amount of physical activity all students do.

Therefore, this will also consist of activities that encourages students to do more exercise. For example, fitness classes, physical activities that do not have an element of competition (e.g. yoga, dance or weights training) and competitive activities that are not as mainstream (e.g. dodgeball, handball or trampolining).

• **Fixtures:** These are an important provision, as it creates an opportunity for students to apply their learnt skills into competition. These teach students about gamesmanship, dealing with success and failure, as well as being a role model for their school.

These also present an opportunity to raise the profile of your school within the community, and further develop students' social skills as they are meeting new people.

An important consideration is the time that this provision can take. For example, in the summer term, cricket fixtures will be required for your students. This will generally begin after-school, as daylight will no longer be a contributing factor – and these fixtures can last a significant amount of time.

You must also consider the location of these fixtures. National competitions tend to begin relatively local, but as your team progresses in the competition, you will be required to travel further to fulfil your fixtures.

Fixtures and competitions also present additional responsibilities that will need to be completed:

- Emergency contacts for all students
- Medical/dietary information for students
- Parental permission
- Booking transportation
- Communication with opposing school
- Providing referees (for home fixtures – if required)
- Preparing pitches (for home fixtures – markings, nets, etc.)
- Washing/preparing team kit
- Ensuring an adequate first aid kit is taken.

• **Trips/visits:** It is very common for schools to provide additional trips and visits related to our subject. These can be to extend students' knowledge, engage students in physical activity or form additional competitions for sports teams.

Trips such as ski trips, sports tours or school exchanges often call upon PE staff to support due to our experiences in practical settings.

- **Risk assessments**: For all of the above, it may be appropriate for you to complete a risk assessment.

There will be a member of staff in the school responsible for this, but as a lead teacher on a trip/visit, you will be required to contribute to this.

There should be a generic risk assessment present for fixtures, but it is worth checking this to ensure you are aware of protocols in case of an emergency.

- **First aid**: It is not essential that a PE teacher holds a valid, and up-to-date first aid qualification. However, it is very advantageous to have a good level of knowledge in how to deal with first aid instances if required.

One of the most common 'mishaps' in our subject area are injuries. Some of the activities we are due to teach within the curriculum have high risk elements, for example, scrums in rugby.

Therefore, appropriate knowledge on how to deal with these instances (if they occur) will be important. Particularly when you may be off-site on a fixture or trip.

Unexpected problems

Within your teaching career, you will be faced with many ups-and-downs. But there are some eventualities that can occur to a PE teacher that were probably not discussed as part of our training.

Here are a few examples of some problems which can occur, and some possible solutions for you to consider.

Students not picked for school sports team

Within secondary schools, mainstream sports clubs can be very popular, particularly in large schools.

Consider your first week in your new school, and you have been asked to run the Year 7 football or netball team. Your opening extra-curricular training session attracts 40+ students, and you need to select a team to compete in a fixture the next week – there will be many students disappointed with your team selection, as well as students that will feel proud to be representing their school.

It is important to communicate to the students that your first team will not be exclusive. This may include a plan to rotate players and give everyone the opportunity to represent the team.

At this stage, your challenge will be to continue to engage the students that are not selected at first. This could be solved by releasing team sheets for your first few fixtures to include a larger number of students. It may also be possible to provide 'B' or 'C' teams for some sports to allow a larger number of students to participate.

It has also been known for some parents/guardians to feel frustrated or disappointed when their child is not selected for a school team. If this occurs, it is important to communicate with them, preferably in person or via a telephone call to ensure the student's confidence is not affected.

Students forgetting kit

This is probably the most common occurrence in most secondary school PE, and is often a genuine mistake from students – but how do you plan to deal with these issues?

Your department may have kit available that students can borrow which will solve this issue on most occasions – but this is only a short-term fix.

It is important to have a clear, and fair, procedure for students that forget items. This is to include sanctions, where necessary, and what is expected of the student for them to borrow the kit for their lesson.

Remember, it is the student's responsibility to bring in the items required for their lesson, as it is in any other lesson.

Injuries

It is important to understand the protocols in place within your school for injuries. Most injuries can be dealt with easily, but may require a trained first aider.

In which case, it is important to keep with you a means of contacting the appropriate, identified person for support. However, this is not always possible from the bottom of the sports field.

Sending a couple of reliable students into the school to get support is an effective way to deal with this situation, and keeps you in a position to reassure the injured student and supervise the rest of the class.

However, it is important to analyse the situation carefully before taking action. For example, if there is a chance of a broken bone, it would be very unwise to try and move the student – so keeping them still and supported will be your main priority while you wait for support.

Transport delays

Due to the volume of fixtures you will need to fulfil, it is possible that you may encounter some transport delays when travelling to, or from an away fixture.

It is common for most students to have a mobile phone – and you may feel it is appropriate for them to use it to contact people who are collecting them to inform them of any delay.

It is also important that you carry a mobile phone with you for these away fixtures too. This will allow you to make contact while away from your school, and communicate with others if delayed or any other issues arise.

Poor weather

This is bound to occur at some point during your first year in your new role – make sure you know the departmental policy for poor weather.

In most schools, lessons will continue unless it causes the activity being taught to be unsafe. Your teaching plan may need to be adapted.

For example, if you are due to teach contact rugby and the ground is frozen, it would be inappropriate to continue with the lesson – there may be alternative activities you can do outside still, if you deem it to be safe.

It is worth having a number of 'poor weather' contingencies planned in case you need them, and you may need to prepare activities for large numbers if more than one class is affected by the bad weather.

The key principle in these instances is to ensure the students' safety at all times.

CHAPTER SUMMARY

Below are a number of 'Top Tips' for you to consider as you start your first year in teaching:

1. **Communication**: Make sure that you communicate with students, colleagues and families effectively. Emails can be useful, but are no substitute for face-to-face conversations, so it is worth considering how to communicate most effectively.

2. **Ask for help**: Be sure to ask for support from your department when required – they have all been in your situation and will have a number of experiences that can help you. Remember you will also be allocated a mentor in your first year, so be sure to use them.

3. **Behaviour issues are not always a reflection**: It is easy to reflect on bad behaviour negatively and attribute it to yourself as the teacher. Students may arrive at your lesson frustrated as a result of something completely

unrelated to you, or your lesson – so try not to be over critical.

4. **Keep up with paperwork**: Try not to leave marking and reports to the last minute. Most schools have an assessment policy that will dictate the time in which you need to provide students with their feedback – but try not to leave it until it is due.

5. **Plan for your future**: As you continue your career, you may be presented with opportunities to progress. It is worth seeking experience in a variety of roles to ensure you make informed decisions about where your career will progress to.

6. **Work–life balance**: Make sure you build in time for personal things. Do not spend every minute of every day working – this will lead you to 'burn out'. Set aside time each week to go out with your friends/family, or do something you enjoy (e.g. going to the gym) – this will break the rhythm of the working week and force you to 'switch off'.

7. **Innovation**: Do things differently, be confident to try new things with your teaching. If things work, be sure to share your practice with your colleagues.

8. **Be reflective**: Reflect after each lesson, consider what worked well and what you could have done differently. You will not always teach 'the perfect lesson', so be sure to take the good components of lessons, and try and develop your practice.

9. **Be strict, but fair**: Your students will be trying to get to know you at the beginning, be sure to be firm with your expectations, and use the school/department sanctions policy where necessary.

10. **Enjoy your teaching**: Remember the reasons you wanted to join this profession, you will have ups-and-downs, but try to enjoy your role and the impact you will have to the students you teach.

Recommended reading

Teaching

Ginnis, P. (2002) *The Teacher's Toolkit*. Crown House Publishing.
The author has complied a number of teaching strategies which can be applied to your planning. Ideas generally encourage students being independent, and strategies to increase engagement/motivation.

Grout, H. and Long, G. (2009) *Improving Teaching and Learning in Physical Education*. Open University Press.
Aimed at teaching trainees in PE, this book reflects on a number of topics relevant to the training year, such as planning, assessment and feedback. It is easy to read, with a number of applied examples within the classroom.

Cohen, L. Manion, L. and Morrison, K. (2010) *A Guide to Teaching Practice*. (Fifth Edition) Routledge.
A useful companion for any initial teacher training course. This book covers a number of basic teaching skills generally, but can be applied to PE teaching with ease.

Wallace, I. and Kirkman, L. (2014) *Talk-Less Teaching: Practice, Participation and Progress*. Crown House Publishing.
The volume of input from a teacher can significantly affect the effectiveness of a lesson. This book includes a number of ideas without large amounts of teacher input.

Griffith, A. and Burns, M. (2012) *Outstanding Teaching: Engaging Learners*. Crown House Publishing.

216

The authors of this book have a proven track record within teacher training. This book provides insights into methods to increase engagement of students, which includes a number of practical examples that can be applied within your lesson planning.

Rodgers, B. (2012) *You Know the Fair Rule: Strategies for Positive and Effective Behaviour Management and Discipline in Schools.* (Third edition) Pearson.

This author is well-known for their insights into behaviour management within the classroom. This book gives a practical guide to behaviour management strategies, and contains a number of practical examples.

Dixie, G. (2011) *Ultimate Teaching Manual.* Bloomsbury.

This book is aimed at newly qualified teachers. It is full of colour-illustrations, and makes use of 'Highway Code' style road signs to help teachers navigate the profession.

PE/sport

Syed, M. (2011) *Bounce: The Myth of Talent and Practice.* Fourth Estate, UK.

This book explores the impact of practice on the development of top athletes. It challenges a number of myths related to sports coaching, and can be very easily applied to teaching within Physical Education.

Epstein, D. (2014) *The Sports Gene: Talent, Practice and the Truth About Success.* Yellow Jersey.

How do athletes excel? And to what extent can their bodies be stretched? This book explores the age-old debate of nature vs nurture, with a number of useful considerations for teaching PE.

Coyle, D. (2010) *The Talent Code: Greatness Isn't Born. It's Grown.* Arrow.

Can ability be created or nurtured? Or is it a fixed power from birth? This book considers how talent can be developed by approaching tasks in different ways. The author makes reference to research undertaken within a tennis academy, while also revealing he feels some teaching methods can be more effective than others.

Coyle, D. (2012) *The Little Book of Talent.* Random House Books.

An extension to the author's previous book: *The Talent Code*, this book gives a number of applied practical tips that can be used to improve skill development. A number of these examples are general, but can be easily applied to teaching PE.

Recommended reading

Ankersen, R. (2015) *The Gold Mine Effect: Crack the Secrets of High Performance*. Icon Books Ltd.
This author is a former professional athlete, who quit his job to research questions such as: 'Why have the best middle distance runners grown up in the same Ethiopian Village?'. The book raises some interesting conclusions and insights into developing sporting talent.

Capel, S. (2015) *Learning to Teach Physical Education in the Secondary School*. (Fourth Edition) Routledge.
This book gives insights into a number of basic teaching skills aimed at the initial teacher training process. This book is specifically aimed at PE teachers, and is part of a series with a range of other subjects.

Subject knowledge

Schmidt, B. (2015) *Volleyball: Steps to Success* (part of the Steps to Success Activity Series) Human Kinetics, Australia.
This is one example of the series that provides a vast number of practical drills and ideas which can be applied to your planning. Editions are available in most mainstream sports. They are very valuable resources to improve subject knowledge in activities you may be less knowledgeable.

Pearson, A. (2007) *SAQ Football: Training and Conditioning for Football*. (Second Edition) A&C Black Publishers Ltd.
This is another example of a book from a series, that is full of practical drills and ideas which can be applied to your lesson planning. This book includes a number of short fitness activities which can be applied to football, or within generic warm up activities.

Kovacs, M. (2010) *Dynamic Stretching: The Revolutionary New Warm-up Method to Improve Power, Performance and Range of Motion*. Ulysses Press.
The title of this book is slightly misleading, but what it does include is a wide number of dynamic stretching activities which can be used to provide some variety to your practical warm ups.

Davis, R. Bull, R. Roscoe, J. and Roscoe, D. (2000) *Physical Education and the Study of Sport*. (Fourth Edition) Mosby.
This textbook provides a comprehensive coverage of the knowledge required for examination PE up to Key Stage 5. It includes a number of diagrams and illustrations, and would be the perfect companion for

improving subject knowledge related to teaching the theoretical aspects of the subject.

Resources

Bizley, K. (2016) *AQA GCSE Physical Education: Student Book.* (Third Edition) OUP Oxford.
These books are designed for teaching GCSE PE from September 2016. It includes a comprehensive coverage of the theory content required for GCSE examinations. Alternative texts are available for different examination boards.

CGP Books. (2016) *New GCSE Physical Education Complete Revision & Practice – for the Grade 9–1 Course.* Coordination Group Publications Ltd (CGP).
This is a popular resource for students to use independently to support revision and preparation for their GCSE PE examination. Illustrated well, and includes a basic explanation of theoretical concepts.

Useful websites

Teachpe.com
A comprehensive website which includes resources, theory content for teaching and practical coaching ideas within a number of activities. This site also includes a number of relevant blogs, useful for both teachers and students.

Afpe.org.uk
The home of The Association for Physical Education (afPE). This site includes latest news relevant to PE and school sport. You will also be able to find information regarding becoming a member, which will also give you access to some additional resources and support.

www.bbc.co.uk/education
GCSE Bitesize is an online resource aimed to support students' revision for examinations. It can be useful to direct students to this site for research or revision tasks.

Journals.humankinetics.com
This site will be able to direct you to the *Journal of Teaching in Physical Education.* This will list a number of research papers, academic journals, and studies related to teaching PE.

Index

Index

Index

Index